COMPLIMENTARY
BONUS GIFT
($2,500 VALUE)

MW00463448

Claim Your Free FAST Coaching Experience with Dr. Keith Johnson!

You are invited to an exclusive coaching session to discover the #1 brake STOPPING you from accelerating to your fullest financial potential.

Finally, accomplish more in an INSTANT than you ever could trying to earn a paycheck, save for retirement, or get out of bad debt.

Ready to get REAL results FAST?

**Register at
FastCoachingExperience.com
to receive NOW!**

DR. KEITH JOHNSON

FINANCIAL FAST TRACK

HOW TO EXPERIENCE ABUNDANCE, ACCELERATE RESULTS, ELIMINATE BAD DEBT

INSPIRE

For foreign and subsidiary rights, contact the author.

ISBN: 978-1-954089-90-7   1 2 3 4 5 6 7 8 9 10

Printed in the United States of America

CONTENTS

Preface 11

Introduction: Get on the Fast Track 15

   CHAPTER 1. Want Wealth in a Wheelchair?
   How Eleven Days Can Take Forty Years 23

FINANCIAL FAST TRACK #1 41

   CHAPTER 2. The Infinite Imagination 43

   CHAPTER 3. ImagineAction 61

   CHAPTER 4. Release the Emergency Brake 77

   CHAPTER 5. Push the Accelerator! Get Clear on What You Want 89

FINANCIAL FAST TRACK #2 103

   CHAPTER 6. Elevate Your Value:
   Be More Generous, Serve More of God's Children 105

   CHAPTER 7. Five Decisions to Elevate Your Value:
   Leaving the Cult of Mediocrity 119

FINANCIAL FAST TRACK #3 135

   CHAPTER 8. Level 10 Relationships:
   Establishing Your Million-Dollar Roundtable 137

FINANCIAL FAST TRACK #4 153

   CHAPTER 9. Owning and Paying Yourself First:
   Expand Your Opportunity Fund to Become an Investor 155

FINANCIAL FAST TRACK #5 167

   CHAPTER 10. Multiply Your Income and Build a Lake of Wealth 169

FINANCIAL FAST TRACK #6 183

   CHAPTER 11. Leverage OPR to Increase Assets:
   Build Wealth and eliminate Liabilities 185

FINANCIAL FAST TRACK #7 205

   CHAPTER 12. Mind Your Business: Buy, Start, Grow, Scale, and Sell 207

   CHAPTER 13. The Solomon Strategy 221

   CHAPTER 14. My $83,000-a-Month Secret: What's Next for You? 229

ACKNOWLEDGMENTS

First, I want to celebrate all the voices who have had the guts to talk about the subject of money and wealth. Even if I disagree with you, I want to thank you for your courage, passion, and compassion to help others build their financial intelligence.

I want to thank Jerret Hammons for helping me to stay on track for more than two years to get this book and training material completed. You know how to capture my thoughts so that people can accept them, digest them, and be changed by them.

A special thanks to Donna Scuderi. Your finishing touches and editorial work took this book from good to great. Your help took me from being happy about the book to feeling proud of the book.

A special thank you to fashion photographer Natalia Aguilera from Miami, Florida for making the vision of the cover picture a reality.

PREFACE

There I was, the proverbial kid in a candy store. But this candy store was a mile and a half of asphalt. My candy? A Velocity Yellow Corvette Z51—my dream car. Our Corvette club had driven from Tampa to the Atlanta Motor Speedway, and I was ready to burn rubber.

I have always loved speed. When I was ten years old, my dad was coming to pick me up for the weekend. I waited and waited. Disappointed that he was late and sure that he'd forgotten about me, I went back inside and dialed his house. There was no answer.

Moments later, a black-on-black Corvette Stingray pulled into the driveway, horn honking. I stared in shock and disbelief as my dad emerged from the driver's seat. My only thought was, *That car is a bad Mama Jama. I want one of those when I get my license!*

From that moment on, I wanted a Corvette of my own.

Now, in Atlanta, I sat in the cockpit of my own Z51. My instructor said, "Forget everything you know about driving. To do high speeds on a fast track like this one, you have to operate differently."

He explained that on the streets, you are expected to drive at or below posted speed limits. But there are no speed limits on a racetrack. You're supposed to accelerate beyond your perceived limitations. If you don't, it can be fatal. And if you make a mistake, you don't slow down. You correct your course as you accelerate through it. The same is true when you see an accident ahead. On the interstate, you mash the brakes, but on the racetrack you either accelerate past the wreck or risk becoming a casualty.

I learned on the racetrack that speed cures all. So, I gripped the wheel at nine and three and did as I was told.

The Financial Fast Track

The speed lesson from the racetrack also applies to wealth-building. I call it the *Financial Fast Track*. People often ask me, "Why the emphasis on *fast*? Don't slow and steady win the race?"

In short, no. Soon, I will show you exactly why going slow is not only detrimental to your financial health, but a proven formula for failure.

|||||||||||||||||||||||||||||||||| **FINANCIAL FAST TRACK FACT** ||||||||||||||||||||||||||||||||||

GOD, SUCCESS, AND MONEY LOVE SPEED.

Have you ever been in a bad place financially? I have—a few times. When you are stuck, all you want is to get out fast. That's a good thing. You can't afford to accept failure. Never try to make sense of something that is less than your potential. If you stay in a negative place, you'll soon become accustomed to it.

Today, one of the hardest and most crippling places you can be financially is in the comfort of a middle-class lifestyle. It's one of the scariest compromises you can make. A few years ago, I lay in the hospital recovering from emergency heart surgery. It was a lifesaving procedure requiring a fourteen-day stay. To be honest, I was afraid to be discharged and sent home. I felt comfortable and safe where I was.

When my doctor offered a choice between being discharged on Friday or staying until Monday, I asked my nurse what he thought. Instantly, he said, "Keith, you don't belong here. You need to go home and recover. The hospital is the most dangerous place for you. There are germs floating everywhere. It's not as safe as you think."

When I realized the hospital was the wrong place, I wanted to get out as fast as I could—like the time I got off the plane in California and accidentally walked into the women's restroom. I couldn't get out fast enough!

You might be in a dangerous place financially. Maybe you have been there so long that it feels comfortable. My friend, get out of there *fast*. It could be fatal to your future!

Comfortable is not what you need. Here's something else you don't need: another book on how to become the "millionaire next door."[1] And you don't need

---

1 Thomas J. Stanley and William D. Danko, *The Millionaire Next Door: The Surprising Secrets of America's Wealthy* (New York: Simon & Schuster, 1996).

a Christian financial advisor telling you how to scrimp, save, and play small. Eating beans and rice and selling your wagon to get out of debt are strategies from the Agricultural Age and Industrial Revolution. They are covered with dust and haven't worked since at least the 1980s.

Why? Because they don't take into account the current speed of change.

"Okay, Dr. J. What are the seven baby steps I can take to fast-track my money and get out of debt?"

Listen, you don't need seven little baby steps to get out of debt. Do you want baby money, or do you want generational wealth? What you need to take are massive, quantum leaps. And if you want to become wealthy in this lifetime, you need to understand that borrowing is not your enemy. It is a tool and a weapon for wealth creation.

You might be reading this and thinking, *Man, this guy is all about prosperity. I'm not sure this message is theologically balanced. He sounds kind of greedy.* Make no mistake—if you are not on track to leave a significant inheritance for your children's children, *you* are greedy and selfish, and you are sacrificing your family on the altar of Mammon.

If hearing that ignites your engine, welcome to the Financial Fast Track and the seven tracks I have identified to experience abundance, accelerate results, and eliminate bad debt!

FINANCIAL
FAST TRACKS

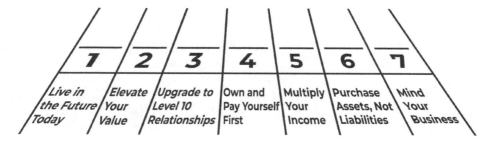

1	2	3	4	5	6	7
Live in the Future Today	Elevate Your Value	Upgrade to Level 10 Relationships	Own and Pay Yourself First	Multiply Your Income	Purchase Assets, Not Liabilities	Mind Your Business

These concepts work. How soon they work for you depends on how quickly you quit believing and behaving like 95 percent of the middle class. It also depends on how committed you are to the process. Look, my Z51 can go from static to 60 mph in under three seconds—the same three seconds it takes to get on the fast track to becoming a millionaire!

Does that sound crazy to you? It's not.

It takes only three seconds to decide whether you want generational wealth.

It takes only three seconds to imagine it.

It takes only three seconds to start storing it.

It takes only three seconds to invest it.

And it only takes only three seconds to give it.

So, are you ready to jump on the track and forget everything you know about money and debt? If you are, congratulations!

The only thing left to say is, "Ladies and gentlemen, start your engines."

INTRODUCTION:
GET ON THE FAST TRACK

D o you feel like you should be much further along financially than you are? If so, you are further behind than you think. Need proof? If you have worked twenty years at $50,000 per year, you have already made a million dollars. But are you a millionaire?

No? So where did all that money go?

The problem isn't that you don't make enough money. The problem is that you don't make it fast enough. The cold, hard truth is that you are *way* behind where you should be financially.

» You shouldn't be paying for a college degree you're not using.

» You shouldn't be fighting to keep a job you hate.

» You shouldn't be deep in credit card debt with nothing to show for it.

» You shouldn't owe more on your car than it's worth.

» You shouldn't be dumping money into a house that isn't paying you.

» You shouldn't still be arguing with your spouse about money.

Zig Ziglar has been quoted as saying, "Money isn't the most important thing in life, but it's reasonably close to oxygen on the 'gotta have it' scale."[2]

He was right. Money isn't everything, but it affects your life and the people you love. If you are behind financially, you just need new information, ideas, strategies, and decisions to get yourself on the Financial Fast Track.

If you feel morally obligated to get ahead faster, I wrote this book for you. It isn't for the critical or comfortable who want to coast in life. The ideas, strategies, and secrets I am about to share will save you years of struggle and unnecessarily hard work in achieving your new financial goals.

---

2 "Zig Ziglar Quotes," *BrainyQuote*, accessed September 20, 2021, https://www.brainyquote.com/quotes/zig_ziglar_173503.

However, before I go any further, know this: I have been exactly where you are—feeling behind, stressed, discouraged, and fearful because I knew I was financially vulnerable. I found my way into that spot, and by the grace of God, I found the way out.

||||||||||||||||||||||||| **FINANCIAL FAST TRACK FACT** |||||||||||||||||||||||||

YOUR HISTORY IS A SNAPSHOT OF YOUR FUTURE WITHOUT MASSIVE CHANGE IN THE PRESENT.

How Did This Happen to Me?

Have you asked yourself how you ended up where you are? It's a great question, and there's a simple answer: it happened the same way it happens to all of us.

I did everything my parents, teachers, and preachers taught me about achieving "financial freedom." Yet, despite my hard work and sincere efforts to live godly and provide for my family, I experienced a total financial crash.

It was humiliating. I was strapped by $180,000 worth of bad credit card debt. I owed $20,000 more on my old beat-up car than it was worth. And when the September 11, 2001 terrorist attacks brought America to a standstill, I lost my speaking business.

My wife Bonnie and I had no money in the bank. We had maxed out thirty-nine credit cards and had nowhere to turn. Our relatives were barely getting by, so we couldn't ask them for money. Truth be told, most of them would have been shocked to learn that we were broke. Our credit card spending gave the impression that we were rich.

It was one big façade.

Our financial crash forced us into the most gut-wrenching and humbling choice of our lives: either live homeless or move into my mother-in-law's twelve-by-twelve spare bedroom. If you're not living in your mother-in-law's spare bedroom, just look up and say, "Thank You, God!"

It was the absolute worst season of my life. I was mentally, emotionally, and physically worn out from years of stress and failed attempts to move ahead. I was so low that I told my wife she deserved better and was stupid for marrying me. I even thought, *Maybe she would be better off if I killed myself.* I had confidently taught that "money doesn't make you happy," but I discovered that poverty doesn't make you happy either. It does the opposite. So, in the middle of my financial crisis, I knew that (1) I had to make a drastic change, and (2) unless things changed quickly, my marriage and future finances would only deteriorate.

Lying on my back and staring at the popcorn ceiling, I asked myself a painful but empowering question: *What if everything I learned about money in church, school, and the American culture is wrong?* That moment was the catalyst for where I am today. Clearly, my old thoughts about money were not working for me or for the people who taught me that garbage. And they sure weren't working for most of the people I knew.

So, here's my question: "Have your thoughts about money been working for you?" No?

Then it's time to tell yourself the truth—not fiction or fantasy, but the facts. Just admit, "No, it hasn't been working. And that's how I got here."

FINANCIAL FAST TRACK FACT

THE STARTING BLOCK OF YOUR FINANCIAL TURNAROUND IS THE MOMENT YOU ADMIT YOU ARE WRONG.

Owning up changed my trajectory. During that difficult year, I realized that I didn't need to learn more stuff. I needed to unlearn much of what I had been taught. The same is probably true for you. So much of what we hear involves cute little buzzwords that move us in the moment but never go deep enough to uproot what's preventing our financial transformation.

Motivation and inspiration are great, but they aren't enough. If you motivate idiots, they'll keep doing dumb things. You can inspire them to just feel good, embrace their stupid mistakes, and avoid the discomfort of change. As the saying in Hollywood goes, "You can die from encouragement." When a thousand people keep telling you how wonderful you are, self-deception becomes your eventual demise.

To get onto my Financial Fast Track, I first needed to get off the motivation and inspiration merry-go-round that kept me repeating my mistakes. It was time to learn the facts about finances. As my book *What You Call a Crisis, God Calls a Classroom* explains,[3] I needed to take educated actions toward building a financial fortress that external crises would not destroy.

Money and motivation have their place, but neither will cure poverty or middle-class living. You accelerate change by coupling sound education with massive relevant actions. Printing money and giving it to the poor and middle classes is not the answer. Until they become financially astute, the money that government prints will keep ending up in rich people's hands.

Knowledge is key. The phrase, "What you don't know won't kill you," is a very potent lie. What you don't know can drain your bank account, cripple your health, destroy your marriage, bankrupt your business, and end your career. Millions of the nicest, sweetest people in the world are struggling financially because of what they don't know.

If you don't know the facts, which solutions will you try when financial trouble comes? I'll tell you which ones: the same ones you have used for years—the ones that put you where you are right now.

> *My people are destroyed for lack of knowledge.*
> —Hosea 4:6 (KJV)

Disgust and the Cost of Not Knowing

In my financial seminars I ask, "What is your number one expense this year?" I get all kinds of answers from house, car, and credit card payments to college loan and health insurance costs. But nobody ever guesses their *biggest* expense. That's a problem because until you identify it, you won't acknowledge the pain it causes. Even worse, you will never unleash the number one emotion that can change your life.

That emotion is *disgust*.

Yes! Disgust is the most powerful emotion a human being can experience. The day you say, "I've had it! I am not putting up with this anymore!" is the day your life and financial future will change forever.

So, what is your number one expense?

I'll tell you: it is not knowing how to make a million dollars a year. Think about it: if you made $80,000 last year, your lack of knowledge cost you $920,000.

---

3 Keith Johnson, *What You Call a Crisis, God Calls a Classroom* (Spring Hill, FL: KJI, 2018).

Are you mad yet? I hope so!

A breakthrough can change the course of your life and ensure that it will never be the same. What breakthrough requires most of all are the confidence and courage not to settle for less. When you are disgusted, your financial turnaround doesn't have to take forever. You don't need bogged-down strategies that are preached as gospel truth. You don't have to keep thinking *slow*. The Financial Fast Track is about accelerated results and discovering what you don't know.

When I was trapped in my mother-in-law's house, I was disgusted! I wasn't looking for slow and steady. I needed gigantic, exponential, quantum leaps to get caught up. Even nature teaches us through the power of a simple seed that exponential growth and multiplication are the natural order of things.

If you would have scanned my bookshelves during that time, you would have found hundreds of movies and albums that helped me cope with the pain of my unfulfilled potential. Next to them were stacks of books on spirituality and marriage. What I lacked were good books directly related to building my financial intelligence. Sadly, the ones I had were written by preachers who had no serious money or got what they had by begging for offerings on cable TV.

Listening to them left me miserable, broke, and full of questions.

FINANCIAL FAST TRACK FACT

A MIND FILLED WITH UNANSWERED QUESTIONS IS A MIND FULL OF DOUBT. A MIND FULL OF SOLUTIONS IS A MIND FULL OF CONFIDENCE.

Musts for a New Money Mindset

To begin my search for a genuine financial breakthrough, I established three criteria to test any new money-related belief system:

1) First, it had to check out spiritually.

2) It had to be psychologically sound.

3) It had to be proven practically.

In my twenty years of research since then, I have discovered that most of our wrong thinking about money comes from our religious roots. The dominant religion in the United States is Christianity, but every nation has its dominant faith and money mindsets.

Forming a new mindset forced me to start fresh with the Scriptures. So, I tuned out the TV preachers and read the Bible from cover to cover. I had to see for myself what it said about wealth. I did not cherry-pick a couple of verses and build a belief system on them. I had seen too many people (even preachers) do that. Instead, I considered the Scriptures in their full context.

I also started reading hundreds of biographies and business books from high achievers. I read with a healthy skepticism, however, watching for any evil and dishonest practices they may have used to manipulate and steal from people. What I discovered humbled me. The wealthiest men and women in the world predominately used ancient biblical principles to obtain their success.

For the record, I studied more billionaires than millionaires, believing that if you are going to study people, you should study the best. I was also fortunate to have coached a billion dollar sales producer. By simply hanging around him, I learned how the affluent think. Recently, I was invited to a meeting that cost $10,000 to attend. Every twenty minutes, billionaire after billionaire shared their principles and the up-to-date strategies they used to become wealthy. The benefits of attending that meeting were priceless!

Back to That Empowering Question

My friend, learning new things means being willing to unlearn some old ones. So, let's consider an expanded version of the question I posed earlier: what if everything you have ever learned about money, finances, wealth, work, the rich, the poor, the middle class, and God is 100 percent wrong? Even if some of it is right, are you still missing key pieces of the puzzle?

What I'm asking is for you to entertain some healthy skepticism (aka "doubt") about what you have learned. It takes some confidence to do that. If what you learned isn't working for you, either God is a liar, or you were trained to believe and behave wrongly. Either way, you need to know.

I'm convinced that if I'm not getting results, I must change my belief systems to experience the abundant life God offers. King Solomon experienced that kind of life and became one of the five wealthiest men in world history. As king, he received twenty-five tons of gold as tribute for each of the forty years of his reign (1 Kings 10:14, NLT). Some calculate the total amount to be worth $64.3 billion in today's money.[4] Along with the riches he amassed from taxation, trade, and consulting for kings and queens, Solomon's fortune may have surpassed $2 trillion! (In chapter 13, we will see how he did it.)

Solomon's secret to wealth-building can be summed up in one ancient text: "Through wisdom a house is built, and by understanding it is established; by knowledge the rooms are filled with all precious and pleasant riches" (Proverbs 24:3–4). Solomon's life reveals that our pursuit of success should be a pursuit for wisdom, which provides everything we need to be wealthy, healthy, and happy.

A Great Start

As Solomon showed us, the starting place is to gain *knowledge*, which I define as "current and relevant information." So, congratulations are in order. You are taking that first step by investing in knowledge through the Financial Fast Track.

Your second step is to absorb that knowledge through repetition, which adds to your understanding (or comprehension). The third and most important step is to use this information by taking the right actions. That is true wisdom!

Both your time and your life are precious. The biggest waste of time is to spend years or even decades trying to achieve what you could have done in a year, or a month. You absolutely *can* move from poverty to middle-class living, and from the middle class to the wealthy place. And you can do it much more quickly than you ever imagined.

So, get the knowledge. Master the principles. Study the strategies. And in a few years, you won't have to worry about money ever again. Give yourself a clean slate. Have the confidence to doubt what your mind says is true. Test it. Open yourself to new ways of thinking and allow yourself to explore new possibilities.

Lastly, commit to finishing this book. Anyone can start, but winners always finish. It's time to win.

---

4   "Top Ten Richest People of All Time in Human History," *WealthResult.com*, accessed September 20, 2021, https://wealthresult.com/wealth/richest-people-history.

1

WANT WEALTH IN A WHEELCHAIR? HOW ELEVEN DAYS CAN TAKE FORTY YEARS

D
o you remember the story of the Great Exodus? Moses led the Israelites from enslavement in Egypt to the edge of the Promised Land. But an important detail about the journey is often overlooked: "It is eleven days' journey . . . now it came to pass in the fortieth year" (Deuteronomy 1:2–3).

That's no typo. An eleven-day trip turned into forty years of wandering with just enough to cover the Israelites' daily needs.

Does that sound familiar?

Seventy-eight percent of Americans live from hand to mouth and paycheck to paycheck.[5] Instead of creating fulfilling lives, they settle for a self-focused, middle-class existence. Frankly, it stinks, like being crammed in the middle seat on an airplane. Nobody wants to be there, but many people are. The saddest part is that you eventually believe you've found your lot in life. You even convince yourself that you're happy. You'd better be because the miserable middle is where you will likely die.

---

5 "Living Paycheck to Paycheck Is a Way of Life for Majority of U.S. Workers, According to New CareerBuilder Survey," *CareerBuilder* (press release), 24 Aug. 2017, https://press.careerbuilder.com/2017-08-24-Living-Paycheck-to-Paycheck-is-a-Way-of-Life-for-Majority-of-U-S-Workers-According-to-New-CareerBuilder-Survey.

In a way, that's what happened to Moses. The Israelites' story was turning around. Decades of struggle and scarcity were coming to a close. They could see the Promised Land! Their move from the middle seat to first class was straight ahead, and they were excited.

After forty years of complaining to Moses, they celebrated him: "Moses, you are our hero! We made it here because of you! Finally!"

Then—*bam!*—Moses died, in that miserable middle seat.

Work Now, Rich When I'm Aged

You know those stories about working the same job for forty years and retiring with a gold watch? Unfortunately, that is exactly what many people are facing. It's been called a lot of things, but "wealth in a wheelchair" is my favorite.[6]

Here's how it plays out: You get an education, work your butt off, and deny yourself your wants. You try to save money, so you can (hopefully) retire with dignity. You embrace the long, slow process, hoping to reach your promised land in your old age. It seems like a logical strategy until you realize it's not. You're on the proverbial slow boat to China, and a storm can sink you in a hot minute.

Storms come in many forms. Terrorist attacks, economic crashes, and global pandemics wreak havoc on people's wallets and portfolios, even destroying some. The COVID-19 storm should have been a wake-up call. The financial security of millions was compromised, and hitting the snooze button was no longer an option. It was time to make serious changes.

This book is about helping you to get off the slow boat and build a financial battleship the storms of life cannot sink. Scripture tells us that "money is a defense" (Ecclesiastes 7:12). The more money you have, the better protected you are against enemy attacks and financial storms.

━━━━━━━━━━━━━ **FINANCIAL FAST TRACK FACT** ━━━━━━━━━━━━━

WITHOUT MONEY, YOU ARE UNARMED ON THE BATTLEFIELD OF LIFE.

---

6 M. J. DeMarco, *The Millionaire Fastlane: Crack the Code to Wealth and Live Rich for a Lifetime* (Viperion, 2011), 4.

The Great Wealth Transfer

For the record, God has not ordained a forty-year trek to your promised land. God thinks fast. He says, "*Now* faith is" (Hebrews 11:1). People are becoming billionaires and multimillionaires faster than ever before. "The number of Americans who meet the millionaire threshold is set to increase by an average of 1,700 per day for the coming years."[7] And in almost the blink of an eye, the billionaires list has grown to hundreds.

A million dollars isn't cool. You know what's cool? . . . A billion dollars.[8]
—THE SOCIAL NETWORK

Technology certainly plays a part for early adopters, creators, and entrepreneurs who gain massive wealth. Many top-ten billionaires like Jeff Bezos of Amazon, Mark Zuckerberg of Facebook, and Jack Ma of Alibaba are leveraging the internet. Many twenty-first-century tycoons are also reaching the financial stratosphere at early ages. (Later, I will share how leveraging intellectual property is one of the fastest ways to create wealth on the internet.)

Rapid wealth creation is real, but something even more widespread is about to happen. It will be the biggest wealth transfer in history, and it is expected to double previous estimates. Some experts predict that "nearly 45 million U.S. households will transfer a total of $68.4 trillion in wealth to heirs and charity over the course of the next 25 years."[9] That's a huge money move.

Baby Boomers hold the lion's share of that amount.[10] They are the wealthiest generation in American history and will pass their holdings to their heirs in the coming decades. As Proverbs 13:22 says, "A good man leaves an inheritance to his children's children, but the wealth of the sinner is stored up for the righteous."

When those trillions transfer, you want to be strategically positioned to receive them. That means becoming the right person, in the right place, at the right time, with the right vehicle. Make sure that vehicle meets your requirements for speed.

---

7   Feliz Solomon, "1700 People in America Are Becoming Millionaires Every Day," *Fortune*, 22 Nov. 2016, https://fortune.com/2016/11/22/us-millionaire-wealth-inequality/. This is a pre-COVID-19 projection. While the pandemic has negatively affected some, it has created new opportunities for others.

8   *The Social Network*, Columbia Pictures, 2010; "The Social Network (2010): Quotes," *IMDB.com*, accessed October 4, 2021, https://www.imdb.com/title/tt1285016/quotes/?ref_=tt_trv_qu.

9   "The Great Wealth Transfer," *Cerulli Associates*, accessed September 13, 2021, https://info.cerulli.com/HNW-Transfer-of-Wealth-Cerulli.html?utm_source=CNBC&utm_medium=Press%2520Release&utm_campaign=1811%2520High%2520Net%2520Worth%2520PR.

10   Kate Dore, "Are You Prepared for the Tax Impact of the $68 Trillion Great Wealth Transfer? Here Are Some Options to Reduce the Bite," *CNBC*, 12 July 2021, https://www.cnbc.com/2021/07/12/the-great-wealth-transfer-has-a-big-tax-impact-how-to-reduce-the-bite.html.

Wheelchair wealth takes forty years, but you have other, faster vehicle options, like a bicycle, automobile, jet, or rocket.

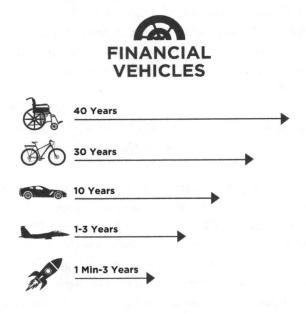

The Evolution of Money

Just as mankind evolved from hunter-gatherers to keyboard jockeys, money has evolved. The speed at which it flows has increased throughout history. It once flowed at the speed of working animals, then advanced to the speed of machinery. More recently, it moved at the speed of telecommunications. Now it moves at the speed of light, from those who value it least to those who value it most and from the poor to the rich. In the future, it will move as quickly as your eyes blink through your virtual glasses.

Money moves faster, and its volume is increasing. Trillions of dollars change hands moment by moment. The laws of physics can help us. According to the second law of thermodynamics, higher-energy objects don't move toward lower-energy objects. Money is a high-energy object, so it loves speed.

Remember the fable of the tortoise and the hare? The hare was quick and spry. The tortoise was persistent and steady but slow. The tortoise won in the end, but in today's economic world (where Amazon Prime can deliver your order in under twenty-four hours) his slow, persistent approach will get you run over. To win today's financial race, you have to be persistent *and* fast!

Fast is the nature of the current age. Decades ago, Intel cofounder Gordon E. Moore predicted that the processing power of computers would double every two years.[11] He had it exactly right, and the American view of speed as a basic value is more evident than ever.

Speed is one reason the United States ranks among the wealthiest nations on earth. Yes! We want everything "microwaved." No! We don't want to wait in line. We want it *now*. That is the American way, and it has produced almost unfathomable results.

Therefore, I can't watch in silence while so many Americans suffer financially. The framework for financial success is here. If you work to maximize your financial literacy and implement your knowledge with great speed, *you will succeed.*

‖‖‖‖‖‖‖‖‖‖‖‖‖‖‖‖‖ **FINANCIAL FAST TRACK FACT** ‖‖‖‖‖‖‖‖‖‖‖‖‖‖‖‖‖

YOU CANNOT CREEP YOUR WAY TO FINANCIAL ABUNDANCE.

The Value of Time

We have all heard that time is money. But is it? Does **time = money**, or is **time > money**?

I believe the second equation is correct. Time is *greater than* money because time is limited. Your life expectancy is roughly eighty years. That gives you only 29,200 days, or 700,800 hours total. However long you live, Father Time is undefeated. The years allotted for making a difference and lots of money are finite.

Any limit on a resource makes it more valuable. We think money is limited, but it really isn't. As long as people and the planet exist, money will be available in some form. In the United States alone, approximately $40 trillion is in circulation,[12] including all physical currency and all funds on deposit in savings and checking accounts. "Money in the form of investments, derivatives, and cryptocurrencies exceeds $1.3 quadrillion."[13]

US currency is the dollar. In Japan, it's the yen, and in Mexico it's the peso. But the currency of earthly life is *time*. The difference between the poor and the

---

11   Carla Tardi, "Moore's Law," *Investopedia*, last updated February 23, 2021, https://www.investopedia.com/terms/m/mooreslaw.asp.

12   "How Much Money Is There in the World?: 2021 Edition," *RankRed*, 28 Aug. 2021, https://www.rankred.com/how-much-money-is-there-in-the-world/.

13   "How Much Money . . . ?"

powerful is their valuation of time. Because they believe time is money, most people work jobs. They trade something of lesser value (money) for something of greater value (time). The rich know that time is infinitely more valuable than money, so they take a different approach. The rich own businesses and seek to create jobs for others (which, by the way, affords them more hours to produce wealth than their workers have).

Your view of time affects how you spend it. I have met many poor and middle-class people who don't value their time. They not only sell it cheaply, but they burn it up on video games, Netflix binges, and televised sports. They habitually trade their most irreplaceable asset for one that can be replenished.

My multimillionaire friends place a high value on their time and don't squander it. The Financial Fast Track will help you do the same. It is about awakening to *possibility*, so you can build big wealth, eliminate bad debts, and leave an inheritance to your descendants. You can't do any of that until you value and protect your time.

I'm not advocating the "slow boat" method because it doesn't work. This book is about *buying back your time* to get the quickest and most profitable outcomes (Ephesians 5:16). To the degree that you devalue your time, you will lack the energy and sense of urgency you need for a fast turnaround. And a fast turnaround is essential!

FINANCIAL FAST TRACK FACT

MAKE THE LARGEST AMOUNT OF MONEY IN THE SHORTEST AMOUNT OF TIME.

Eleven Days? Or Forty Years?

Speed matters. Can you imagine yourself making a million dollars a year? Great. That amounts to $83,333 each month. Lots of people make that kind of money. They made the decision and took massive action. It doesn't have to take forty years. It takes three seconds to decide that you want it. If you're breathing, you still have three seconds to make the choice.

Choosing and reaching the million-dollar threshold was important in building my better future. Imagining a $1 million annual income can light anybody's fire.

But when you imagine $83,333 per month, the dream becomes more concrete and fuels immediate action. You can see the goalpost on the track and drive toward it.

That monthly figure beckoned to me. It spoke of possibility and the speed of money. Then Myron Golden, author of *From the Trash Man to the Cash Man*, told me something that became a bedrock of the Financial Fast Track. He said, "Keith, making a lot of money in a short time is wiser and easier than making a lot of money over a long period."[14]

A week later, I followed his advice and generated $144,351 in one week—in the middle of a pandemic. I remembered the days when I was happy to generate that amount in a year! Now $83,333 a month was no big deal. I could make money even faster than that. It wasn't hard to do, and doing it made me very happy.

That week broke my mind out of financial prison. It was a barrier-busting experience, like when Roger Bannister ran the four-minute mile. No one did it until he proved it was possible. Firsts are important because they change your paradigms. Myron's advice helped me break my personal "four-minute mile." Doing that reset my beliefs about how quickly financial breakthroughs can come.

Myron was right: faster *is* easier!

FINANCIAL FAST TRACK QUESTION

CAN YOU PRODUCE THE SAME INCOME IN A MONTH THAT YOU ONCE PRODUCED IN A YEAR? CAN YOU DO IT IN A WEEK? IN A DAY? (THE ANSWER IS YES.)

Look, if I can accelerate, so can you. You are in the driver's seat. You have what you need to start your engine and choose your path. Easy or hard, quick or slow—you decide. You don't have to choose what the masses choose. You are no longer oblivious to possibility. Remember: I was the guy who thought his wife should dump him. I was busted, broke, and disgusted, and she deserved better. But I'm not that guy anymore. I am living proof that anyone can imagine and choose to act. *Anyone.*

I like what Dr. Joe Vitale says about money and speed:

---

14 Myron Golden shared this during his March 2021 "Make More Offers Challenge."

Money loves speed is an important principle because the people who tend to act the fastest make the most money. When an idea comes to you, you should drop everything and do your best to act on it and complete it and get it to market. You can always revise an idea later, but generally speaking, the first person to bring it to the public is the first person to make the profit. Money loves speed also implies a couple other things. One is that other people are probably getting the same idea as you or something similar. If you don't act on your idea now, somebody else will act on it, and they will profit instead of you.[15]

Dr. Vitale is talking *speed*, and it's exactly opposite to everything you and I were taught. They told us, "Work really hard. Save. Retire wealthy when you get old." Most poor and middle-class people swear by the idea because it was sold to them and the generation before them. But it was never a godly idea.

Consider who benefits from this Industrial Age relic. It keeps working people trading time (more valuable) for money (less valuable). The promise is simple: "Work for us for forty years. We'll give you benefits like paid sick days, vacation, insurance, and a pension, so your family can enjoy financial security after your body wears out. Plus, we'll throw you a retirement party in the break room. We'll give you a pat on the back, a gold watch for your decades of loyalty, and a nice cake with your name on it. Oh—and sorry if the cake's a little dry."

That's what you get for your forty-year journey. (Wait! Where have we heard *that* before?)

FINANCIAL FAST TRACK FACT

WORKING NOW FOR THE FINANCIAL WEALTH YOU'LL ENJOY IN OLD AGE IS A LOSING FORMULA.

Time to Beat That Dead Horse

You won't fully discard a bad idea until you consciously acknowledge its inner workings. What you once accepted at face value must be examined and then trashed. So, yes. We are going to beat that dead horse and then lay it to rest. First, the facts.

---

15   Dr. Joe Vitale, *Money Loves Speed! From Stress to Success, Revealing the Eight Laws of Attracting Money Fast* (Wimberley, TX: Hypnotic Marketing, 2020), xiii–xiv.

Today's workers make the same trade-offs their parents and grandparents made. But the wealth-in-a-wheelchair method is even shakier now than it was then. Modern companies have no sense of loyalty to their employees. No matter how important you think you are to the firm, thousands of other qualified people from all over the world are waiting to take your place.

In this environment, what you decide is critical and depends on what you believe. The first three financial beliefs listed below are from the slow-boat method; the last three are for financial fast-trackers:

» Getting rich easily is stupid and improbable.
» Get-rich-quick schemes must be avoided.
» There's no such thing as "get rich quick."
» Getting rich slowly is risky and dangerous.
» Getting rich quickly is smart and possible.
» Getting rich quickly is easier.

There is a context for both points of view. The slow method is a remnant of agrarian life. To farmers, getting rich quickly was impossible because the growing process was fixed. Farmers determined their proficiency levels and the intended size of their harvests, but they could not tell the ground to hurry up and produce.

In the Industrial Age, many people left the land and took manufacturing jobs. Their income was not limited by nature's dictates but by an agreed-to hourly wage. The only way to make more money was to work overtime or ask for a raise. Workers essentially surrendered to their employers all control over their financial destinies.

This outdated financial strategy was and is comprised of six steps. Studying them will help to expose any embedded belief systems you need to unlearn before you drive the Financial Fast Track. Remember, these are the "rules" most Americans have followed. Therefore, you probably know people who are stuck living with the results.

Step 1: Decide What You Want to Be for the Rest of Your Life

I remember the cultural pressure I felt to make decisions about the rest of my life—as a high school senior! How was that supposed to work? My testosterone levels were soaring, and the farthest ahead I could think was to the next party, where all the beer and girls would be.

Nobody sat me down and assessed my strengths. No one laid out any options. I was confused and clueless and made a stupid decision. It started with a postcard from a technical college in Nashville. I believed that I wasn't smart enough for a university, so I took out a bunch of student loans and attended a one-year school. I figured after that, I could work on greasy engines for about four decades.

Talk about a dumb decision! I could barely change the oil in my own car, much less take out engines and rebuild them. I was a talker, not a hands-on person. Not to mention, I hated getting my hands dirty!

Millions of students have made the same mistake. Without any counsel, and before they are ready, they choose their careers. Then they end up working jobs they hate for the rest of their lives.

This is not a kingdom principle. It is pure cultural pressure. For one thing, your purpose is not a decision. It's a discovery. Purpose comes when you uncover your gifts and identify the problems you are uniquely qualified to solve.

To my younger friends, resist the cultural pressure to decide now. Take time to assess your strengths. Sometimes, you discover them by working different jobs. You might find them by starting a small business. Either way, I believe the purpose of your twenties is to learn what you *don't* want, so you can find your path forward.

Step 2: Get a College Degree

Forbes tells us that "since the 1999–2000 academic year, the net price of tuition, fees, room, and board at a public four-year college has increased by 68%. The amount borrowed to go to college each year has doubled in the same time."[16]

No wonder "the cumulative federal student loan debt is over $1.54 trillion, more than double the amount in 2010"![17] Education is a money-making enterprise, a behemoth that benefits from the wealth-in-a-wheelchair approach. Vast tuition and other revenues give educators power and influence over politicians. Special interest groups support the candidates who promise to keep the higher-education machine well-oiled.

Are you getting the picture?

It is in the best interest of educators to keep the myth going. After all, they profit from it. Don't expect them to offer alternative ideas or courses about how to skip college and build a business instead. If you're asking for a course called "101 Reasons Why College Isn't Necessary," good luck!

The "go to college and get a degree" thought process is so culturally ingrained that young people who decide against it are pegged as rebels, quitters, and even losers. However, a university education is far from the only path to success. Just ask the 30 percent of living billionaires who never earned a bachelor's degree![18]

---

16 Wesley Whistle, "What Is Driving the $1.5 Trillion Student Debt Crisis," *Forbes*, 1 Sep. 2020, https://www.forbes.com/sites/wesleywhistle/2020/09/01/what-drives-the-15-trillion-student-debt-crisis/?sh=391e9b387aec.

17 Wesley, "What is Driving . . . ?"

18 Kathleen Elkins, "Nearly a Third of the World's Billionaires Didn't Graduate College," *CNBC*, 11 Aug. 2016, https://www.cnbc.com/2016/08/11/nearly-a-third-of-the-worlds-billionaires-didnt-graduate-college.html.

I'm reminded of a client whose mother (a doctor) forced her into medical school. After eight years of sacrifice, hustle, and grind, my client stood on the finish line and realized she didn't want to be in medicine. She wanted to be a personal coach for women executives. Unfortunately, she was already saddled with $400,000 in student loan debt, and nearly a decade of her life was gone.

Where might she be today if she had started her own expert empire instead of going to medical school? What if she had invested her energy and that $400,000 building her empire for eight years? Today, she is a graduate of our 83K Academy. She is speaking, coaching, and creating programs that help tired women improve their physical health and boost their energy levels. She is empowering them to maximize their productivity and enjoy life.

Listen, if you want a career in medicine, law, or engineering, college is your path. However, it isn't for everyone, especially if you are called to be an entrepreneur.

Step 3: Get a Job

Another myth lures students into higher education and proves false for 90 percent of graduates. It goes like this: "When you get your degree at our institution, companies will stand in line at your graduation and offer you a six-figure salary."

When you reach the end of that rainbow, reality sets in. There is no shiny pot of gold, and no one waves big money at you. It's all smoke and mirrors, a brilliantly executed sales strategy to attract your dollars to a particular school that makes money off confused, misinformed, and gullible students. When the promise fails, newly minted college grads move back home and work at Chili's to pay down their debt load.

The pressure to go to school and get a "regular job" runs right through our culture. When I lost everything, some family members screamed, "Why don't you get a real job? This ridiculous dream of public speaking isn't going to pay your bills."

Getting a job is the only way most people know to make money and build wealth. They accept the "norm," and tie themselves to jobs they hate. But why would anyone—why would *you*—want to keep trading your time for money? You only have so much time, which means your money will also be limited. And nobody is willing to pay what you are worth anyway.

FINANCIAL FAST TRACK FACT

A JOB IS THE SLOWEST AND WORST WAY TO MAKE MONEY AND BUILD WEALTH.

Why not see your job as a temporary vehicle for building your dreams? Your future financial increase is not connected to your job anyway. It's connected to your dreams. Working for someone keeps you limited to what their potential can produce. You can never exceed their level of success. No wonder most people feel unfulfilled.

I admit, I was often tempted to trade my dream for a "secure" job. But I resisted. I knew a job would give me a paycheck, but my dream would make me a fortune. I'm sure glad I didn't surrender to the barking dogs that hounded me.

> *A salary is the drug they give you to forget your dreams.*[19]
> —KEVIN O'LEARY, *SHARK TANK* STAR

Step 4: Stay Forever for a "Secure Paycheck"

A J-O-B will keep you Just Over Broke, trading the precious commodity of time for a little bit of money, *for the rest of your life.*

The system is designed to give you just enough to pay your bills. But it straps you to the work treadmill, week in and week out. You'll keep giving away your time and money to benefit your boss, the government, and the bankers. You will bury yourself in a growing financial hole.

||||||||||||||||||||||| FINANCIAL FAST TRACK FACT |||||||||||||||||||||||

WORK YOUR JOB FROM NINE TO FIVE BUT WORK YOUR BUSINESS FROM 8 TO 11 AT NIGHT.

Consider this: most people work five days a week and only get paid for one or two days. Monday through Wednesday they make money (1) for the company's benefit, (2) to pay their taxes for the government's benefit, and (3) to pay their credit cards, car loans, and mortgages for the banks' benefit. Technically, they only work Thursday and Friday for their own financial good.

---

19 "A Salary Is the Drug They Give You to Forget Your Dreams—Kevin O'Leary," *Blind*, accessed September 14, 2021, https://www.teamblind.com/post/A-Salary-is-the-Drug-They-Give-You-to-Forget-Your-Dreams"--Kevin-oleary-teenv5Ta.

How can you get ahead by working just sixteen hours a week? It's part of the reason the average family's bills are between $2,000 and $5,000 higher than its annual income.[20]

What you need is to build assets that generate *passive* cash flow—enough to cover your monthly expenses. I'm talking about money that hits your account every week without your having to work for it. That means setting a goal of $5,000, $10,000 or even $83,000 a month in passive income.

If you work from nine to five, make asset building your 8 p.m. to 11 p.m. objective (more about that in chapters 9 and 11). I call it "making money in your underwear." One of the fastest and easiest ways is to create and sell your intellectual assets (more on this in chapters 11 and 13). You're not selling your time but establishing money-makers that will produce income whether you are in bed or at the workplace. This is the opposite of earning a paycheck.

Step 5: Save! Save! Save for Emergencies and Retirement

You know the drill: build up your 401K and pay into Social Security. When you're in your seventies, you might be able to retire or even be wealthy. The outcome is not that predictable, however. What if the stock market crashes? What if Social Security isn't properly funded when the time comes? Have you invested enough to accumulate real wealth?

We have all been taught to "save for an emergency" or "a rainy day." I saved for emergencies and rainy days, and guess what happened? Emergencies and hurricane-level rainy days found me. Why? Because I attracted the object of my focus.

My financial situation started to improve when I changed from saving to *storing*. After all, God promised to bless my storehouse, not my savings. Instead of stashing cash for emergencies, I started storing for future opportunities to make passive income. I started thinking like an investor instead of a saver (more about this in Financial Fast Track #4).

Step 6: Retire in Sunny Florida

If everything goes according to plan, you spend decades in the prison of self-denial, stress, and scarcity-living, and you barely get by. You retire grey-haired, wrinkled, and overweight, having beat up your body with stress and the work you hated. Now you're ready to travel and enjoy the good life.

Yeah, right.

---

20 Grant Cardone talks about this common annual shortfall. It is one of the ways an average family accumulates upwards of $40,000 in credit card debt.

I remember back in the day, standing in line at the bank to cash a check. In the queue beside me was a man in his late seventies. His hearing wasn't great, so he talked loudly enough for everyone to hear his conversation with the teller. Like some older people do, he overshared.

"I need to withdraw $125," he said, "so I can buy some groceries for my wife and me."

The teller checked his account and quietly said, "I am sorry, sir. You only have $36 in your account."

"What?" he asked nicely. "Oh. Okay. I also need to buy medicine for my wife. Just give me $20."

Then the saddest thing happened. The old man looked at me and said, "Well, I guess I'll have to wait two weeks for my Social Security check, so I can get some groceries."

His words brought tears to my eyes. I thought, *Wow! Is this the future you want for yourself—having to decide between groceries and medicine in your old age?* If you follow the masses, the odds are stacked against you. It is highly probable that you will end up like the majority who are on that agonizing path. Their wealth philosophy has failed them, and it will fail you.

Millions of seniors live in abject poverty. I live in Florida, and, trust me, most seniors who bought the lie are just like the man in the bank. Many of them die with zero assets and less than $10,000 to their name—and that includes housing wealth! Some pass away with no money saved at all, leaving their families to cover their funeral expenses.

That is no way to live or die!

Just say *no* to wealth in a wheelchair. Don't be casual about getting on the Financial Fast Track, or you will become a casualty. Of course, it's your decision. You can play now and pay later. Or you can pay now for the life you want and deserve.

Two Stories People Tell Themselves

There are two basic stories (or flat-out lies) people tell themselves about why they can't turn around their finances. Let's take a look.

Story #1: "It's Going to Take Me a Long Time"

Psychologically, we humans run away from pain and toward pleasure. If change is difficult and too slow, we avoid it like the plague. However, when you believe that change can happen in a moment, you are more apt to start the journey.

All changes are created in a moment—it's just that most of us wait until certain things happen before we finally decide to make a shift.[21]
—TONY ROBBINS

Believing in fast change is not folly. The real myth is that changing your financial story takes a lifetime. Don't buy it! I believe all real change happens in a moment. It just takes a while to reach the moment and be ready for it. But once you get there, you will make the tough decisions and experience positive, accelerated change.

Why? Because change happens at the speed of a decision. The speed of your financial decisions determines the speed of your financial breakthroughs.

For your life to change and progress, *you* must change. For your life to get better, *you* must get better. If you don't change in your present, the same failures will follow you into your future. Remember: unless you take massive action now, your financial past is a snapshot of your financial future.

Story #2: "I Don't Have Enough Time; I Am Too Old"

If you are older, it might be easier to feel hopeless and believe that your time is up. You might feel like it's impossible to become wealthy, so why even try? This is called learned hopelessness, a destructive belief system that says, "No matter what action I take, nothing will change. I have tried and failed in the past. Nothing I try will make any difference. The world system, the devil, rich people, and life itself are against me. I can't do anything about it."[22]

When you believe those lies, hopelessness and stress become your permanent dance partners, and confidence bows out. You become passive instead of aggressive, weak instead of strong, and pitiful instead of powerful. They consume you and keep you dwelling on problems and obstacles instead of solutions and possibilities for a quick recovery.

Why not see your financial setbacks as learning experiences? You have learned what doesn't work, so leverage that knowledge! This way of thinking moves you from learned hopelessness into a possibility mindset. Suddenly, each failure takes you closer to a win.

If you are older, you need to know it's not too late. I have coached many clients near retirement age and beyond. Maturity is an asset when writing a book or launching a coaching or consulting practice, for example. After working at the

---

21 Tony Robbins (@TonyRobbins), Twitter, August 17, 2015, 12:08 p.m., https://twitter.com/tonyrobbins/status/633309461306699776?lang=en.

22 Eric Postal, "Learned Helplessness, Learned Hopelessness," *Diagnostic Imaging*, 16. Nov. 2012, https://www.diagnosticimaging.com/view/learned-helplessness-learned-hopelessness.

same place for thirty-five years, one of my senior-citizen 83K Academy students wanted to create more meaning and wealth. I helped him assemble a coaching package, and he took it to his previous employer. Now they pay him more than he earned as their employee, and he spends just a few hours each week coaching younger leaders and throwing ideas at problems.

The best part? He is free to take on more clients to scale beyond six and seven figures. It wasn't too late for him, and it's not too late for you. You already have $1 million worth of intellectual property. You're just not using it.

My Personal Turnaround Story

You know about the deep, dark hole that tried to swallow me in 2002. What felt like the worst year of my life turned out to be one of the best. But did I mention that it forced my ego to shrink?

Yes! I had a big know-it-all ego. I was closed to new ideas about finances and money. After all, I'd heard all the latest "money" sermons, so I thought I was all set. An ego that big is apt to produce a small bank account—and it did! I know now that shrinking your ego can enlarge your bank account.

|||||||||||||||||||||||||||||| **FINANCIAL FAST TRACK FACT** ||||||||||||||||||||||||||||||

IF YOU WANT TO DOUBLE YOUR INCOME, QUADRUPLE YOUR LEARNING.

Throughout this book, I will share seven Financial Fast Track Strategies I used to arrive at my financial promised land. I haven't fully arrived, because there is always another financial mountain to climb. I am also acutely aware that my steps won't work for everybody. As Mark Twain said on his seventieth birthday, "We can't reach old age by another man's road. My habits protect my life, but they would assassinate you."[23]

The Financial Fast Track is not a one-size-fits-all proposition. Your path will be different from mine, and like the Israelites, you have multiple paths available. You can walk a long and winding road, take an in-between pace, or ride the fast track straight to your destination.

---

23 "Seventieth Birthday Speech: Mark Twain, 1905," *PBS*, accessed September 23, 2021, https://www.pbs.org/kenburns/mark-twain/birthday-speech/.

When I decided to change my direction through what I believed, my income doubled for three straight years. That's how quickly you can change course. And with the help of this book, you could experience even faster results than I did.

You can experience abundance, as I did. And you can watch your results accelerate. Bonnie and I left my mother-in-law's house and moved into the home of our dreams: a ranch style mini-mansion. We eliminated our consumer credit card debt. I went on to become a multimillion-dollar expert producer as an international speaker, high-ticket coach, and Amazon best-selling author.

I dropped the wealth-in-a-wheelchair strategy, got off the slow boat to China, and stepped into what felt like a rocket ship. It blasted me into a new financial stratosphere of success and happiness.

Are you ready to do the same?

. . . .

FINANCIAL FAST TRACK COACHING

Your mind is designed to produce ideas, strategies, and solutions *as you place a demand on it.* If you have been conditioned to think financial success is a long, slow road, your mind will find long, slow ways of making it happen.

However, if you place a demand on your mind to create financial success quickly, your mind will search for more efficient ideas and strategies to make it happen. Let these exercises help you get there!

1) Choose the speed at which you want to build wealth and eliminate bad debt.
   [ ] Slow
   [ ] Medium
   [ ] Fast

2) Write down your current annual income. _____
   Whatever the number, it's time to stretch!

   How can you produce in one month what you typically earn in a year?

   How can you produce in one week what you earn in a year?

   How can you produce in *one day* what you earn in a year?

3) Place this demand on your true potential. You are a genius. Imagine bigger, and bigger strategies will follow.

FINANCIAL
FAST TRACK

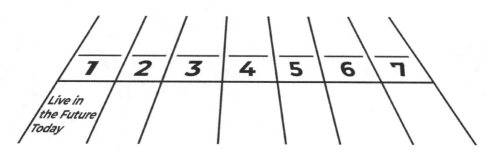

1 | 2 | 3 | 4 | 5 | 6 | 7

Live in the Future Today

2

THE INFINITE IMAGINATION

Being trapped in my mother-in-law's spare bedroom was a rock-bottom experience. I read book after book, searching for answers, strategies, steps, and tactics for becoming a debt-free millionaire-next-door type. I also scoured journals full of sermon notes about sowing miracle seeds, achieving breakthrough, and tithing to create wealth.

But something wasn't adding up. Something was missing.

I lacked the motivation to act and change my situation. When I saw the people who attended the same financial education classes at church that I did, I couldn't help but notice that 99 percent of them never experienced financial change.

Like herds of cattle, they trudged into class, mired in consumer debt and struggling to get ahead. A year later, they were just as broke and indebted. A few twenty-year-olds with no kids or responsibilities got debt free, but that was it. A couple of other attendees who went bankrupt held up their little signs saying that they were debt free too.

But nobody held up signs saying that they had become wealthy. I thought, *Maybe there's a deeper problem here.*

The significant problems we face cannot be solved at the same
level of thinking we were at when we created them.[24]
—ALBERT EINSTEIN

I didn't know where to turn, so I hired a coach—a gentleman who had created the kind of life I felt called to. He was a millionaire, an executive branding and marketing consultant to other millionaire and multimillionaire authors, speakers, coaches, and television personalities whom he had developed in his career. His coaching resume was impressive.

Within a couple of months of working together, he helped me outline my book, which was released by one of New York City's largest publishers. He helped me to craft my original message, which I have shared on stages, reaching over a million people. But on a certain afternoon, he asked a question that became foundational to my success: "Keith, do you want to know the secret of all these big guys?"

Of course I did! Was it their looks, talent, or intelligence? Was it how they communicated through their books? Was it how they dressed and carried themselves during appearances?

It was none of that.

What he said next shocked me. "The secret to their success is that they live in the future *today*."

At first, the idea confused me. Then he broke it down. "All the multimillionaire business owners and celebrities I know used their imagination to see the divine possibilities of who they could be, what they could do and have, and the people they could help in the future. Then they started living it today."

The idea stuck with me. Then, while developing my Financial Fast Track, I heard a parable that permanently transformed my sense of *possibility*. The story goes that a professional golfer was invited to Saudi Arabia to play with the king.[25] The golfer accepted and was whisked away in a private jet. The men golfed for a few days and had an amazing time together.

As the golfer prepared to leave, the king said, "It is customary for me to give my guest a gift as a token of our meeting."

---

24 "The significant problems we face cannot be solved at the same level of thinking we were at when we created them," *Quotes*, accessed September 24, 2021, https://www.quotes.net/quote/9226.

25 Joel Osteen tells the story in *Your Best Life Now* (New York: Warner Faith, 2004), 11–12, but versions of the story have apparently been told since the late 1940s.

The golfer graciously declined, "That isn't necessary. I don't need anything. Just playing here with you was more than enough, my friend. I make a great living doing what I love. I couldn't ask for anything more."

But the king insisted, "It is custom."

The golfer finally agreed, "Okay. I collect golf clubs. So if you must give me something, I would accept that."

The king said, "It is done. I will give you a golf club."

On the flight home, the golfer wondered, "What kind of golf club would a king give me—a diamond-encrusted putter? A driver made of gold?

A few days later, there was a knock on the golfer's door, and a courier delivered an envelope. Inside was the title deed to a golf club—*an entire golf club*. Not a putter or driver, but a club where people play golf!

Your Infinite Possibility Future

Living in the future now begins with imagining the divine, infinite nature of possibility. Simply put, it means thinking how God thinks. John 4:24 says that "God is Spirit." He doesn't think with a mind like we do, he thinks as Spirit.

When someone says, "Think *bigger*," it's not the mind of God. God thinks with His imagination. Therefore, He thinks in terms of the infinite. Scripture describes it this way:

> *"My thoughts are not your thoughts, nor are your ways My ways," says*
> *the Lord. "For as the heavens are higher than the earth, so are My ways*
> *higher than your ways, and My thoughts than your thoughts."*
> —Isaiah 55:8–9

Scripture does not say God thinks bigger; it says He thinks *higher*. His thoughts come from a higher place beyond the mind. It's a place called *spirit*.

⸻⸻⸻⸻ **FINANCIAL FAST TRACK FACT** ⸻⸻⸻⸻

POSSIBILITY COMES WHEN YOU THINK HOW THE KING THINKS.

When you think bigger, your mind expands from your current level of experience. Yet that is a limiting framework. When you think higher, your imagination is required to expand to an *infinite possibility* future. That is an unlimited framework.

Where does this kind of thinking come from, and how do we to tap in?

Well, it isn't in our minds. The mind is a function of the brain, which keeps us from danger. Its purpose is surviving, not thriving. Infinite possibility is different. It begins in the imagination, the part of us that makes us great, like God. The imagination is a function of the spirit.

There is a problem, however, and it began at the fall of humanity. The enemy seduced Adam and Eve and sold them a lie. He persuaded them to focus on the one forbidden tree they "lacked" instead of the *abundance* of other trees to which they had access. God warned them never to eat from the Tree of the Knowledge of Good and Evil, but the enemy knew exactly how to tempt them.

He said, "If you eat from this tree, you'll be like God" (see Genesis 3:5).

My friend, you are not God, but you are like Him. Genesis 1:26–27 says that He created us in His image and likeness. God is a creator, so you are a creator too. That means you can create something from nothing. When others see circumstances, you see solutions. You can take the broken and create something beautiful. The only limitation is in failing to engage your infinite imagination. Remember: the created can never outthink or out-imagine the creator.

Pink Elephants in Africa

Right now, I want you to do something, but it is going to sound strange. Are you game?

Think about a pink elephant in the African jungle. Picture her floppy pink ears and long pink trunk.

What happened? Did you see a pink elephant? Yes. Are there any pink elephants in Africa? No. So where did yours come from?

It came from your imagination, which did what God designed it to do: it created something that has never existed. You acted like God and created a pink elephant. Now do the same, but, instead of a pink elephant, imagine your desired financial future. Create it by engaging your imagination. Let it preview your abundant future *today*, the way a movie preview shows you coming attractions.

That is exactly what I did at my mother-in-law's house. It was my first Financial Fast Track discovery. I'd lost my house, furniture, connections, income, and confidence. The only things I had left were my laptop, a cell phone, and my imagination. Out of disgust and frustration, I slammed the bedroom door and closed my eyes. I used my imagination to see a "future me" and a place that was far beyond where I was. I saw myself as an international speaker with thousands of people listening to me, a best-selling author, a high-ticket coach, and someone who had a million dollars.

With that picture in my present, I lived in my future and shouted, "I am a success in life. I am a best-selling author and travel all over the world speaking to millions of people. I am a millionaire. I am a success."

I stomped. I yelled. I spit. I laughed. But most importantly, I saw a full-color picture of my future, as clear as day in my imagination. Five years later, I was living what I imagined in that tiny room. From that day forward, I took the unseen and showed it to the world—and it happened *fast*.

Did you catch that? I took the unseen and showed it to the world. Your imagination needs to first create and then feed your mind two very important pictures daily:

1) A picture of the abundant future you want to build

2) A picture of the successful mentor you want to become

The Financial Fast Track is not only about your success but about helping others to succeed. When I began to see the unseen, my life changed, and I became of greater service to others.

God created everything out of the unseen, which is the imagination. *Unseen* does not mean "nonexistent." Air is unseen, but it exists. Energy is unseen, but it exists. God created everything from a picture in His imagination. In this way, we are like Him. We are the only species on earth that can imagine something and create it.

Birds build nests. Bees build hives. Beavers build dams. But humans build and create futures. God gifted us with imagination, so we could move *higher* and operate like Him.

FINANCIAL FAST TRACK FACT

YOU ARE A CREATOR OF YOUR FINANCIAL FUTURE, NOT A VICTIM OF YOUR PAST FINANCIAL MISTAKES.

Choose the Dream You Live In

Here's the trap that snares so many: When we aren't living to our full potential, we aren't creating, and we fall victim to the creations of others, whether good or bad. It's that simple. You are either living in your dream or in someone else's.

Here's an example: Americans are currently living in the imagination of Thomas Jefferson, who died almost two hundred years ago. He envisioned what this nation could be and wrote out the framework. His vision isn't the only one we live in, however. Despite our nation's problems, Dr. Martin Luther King, Jr. imagined it as a place where people would judge others according to the content of their character, not their skin color. When Barack Obama became president, we lived a manifestation of Dr. King's imagination.

Dreams work both ways. Adolph Hitler had a dream: to create a state where everyone looked and believed like he did. His dream produced massacres, destruction, and a nightmare of global proportions. Hitler created all of it from his imagination, and the world lived it.

Notice that evil men don't ask God's permission to create what they imagine. Their ideas are not from God, but they dream them anyway. Our godly dreams are different. God is waiting for us to create them. We just need to make sure they are God-breathed and God-sized. Otherwise, we will create dreams that are not from Him.

A good example is the "dream" of wheelchair wealth. Millions have bought into it, have struggled most of their lives, and have regretted it in the end. It wasn't a big dream, but even if it was, it was never enough. The people who told us to dream big never quantified what that means in financial terms. The word *big* is ethereal and subjective. It allows them and us enough wiggle room to avoid accountability for achieving it.

It is time to quit playing with nebulous words and nail down a dollar amount for what *big* looks like.

Are you in?

Place a Demand on Your Imagination

You are entering mind-stretching territory, so keep your mind open and hear me out. If you want change, you must place a demand on your imagination. Don't just think big. Go higher. I'm convinced that God wants next-level financial status for you beyond your current lifestyle. So let me help you to identify some annual income levels that are possible. Wherever you are on this "scale," there is an income level that is higher, and there is a "future you" to match it.

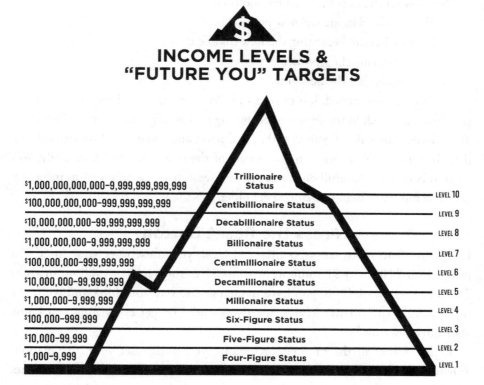

INCOME LEVELS & "FUTURE YOU" TARGETS

$1,000,000,000,000–9,999,999,999,999	Trillionaire Status	LEVEL 10
$100,000,000,000–999,999,999,999	Centibillionaire Status	LEVEL 9
$10,000,000,000–99,999,999,999	Decabillionaire Status	LEVEL 8
$1,000,000,000–9,999,999,999	Billionaire Status	LEVEL 7
$100,000,000–999,999,999	Centimillionaire Status	LEVEL 6
$10,000,000–99,999,999	Decamillionaire Status	LEVEL 5
$1,000,000–9,999,999	Millionaire Status	LEVEL 4
$100,000–999,999	Six-Figure Status	LEVEL 3
$10,000–99,999	Five-Figure Status	LEVEL 2
$1,000–9,999	Four-Figure Status	LEVEL 1

Are you getting this? People are living at eight, nine, and soon to be ten of these levels. The big question is, "Which level is yours?"

Most people today are living at Level 1 or 2, making less than $100K per year. Sadly, most people at the higher end of Level 2 think they have arrived. But if you are on Level 2 of the mountain, you have not "arrived"! Please humble yourself and admit that you might be thinking "putter" instead of imagining "golf club."

Your imagination gives you wings to fly into a future that doesn't exist yet. Most people are mentally trapped in the prison of what is or what was, instead of *what can be*. They're not using their infinite possibility imagination, but using it is mandatory if you want to fly out of your Level 1 or Level 2 prison.

That's especially true in our accelerated world. Have you noticed that nobody talks about "thousands" or even "millions" anymore? Ten or twenty years ago, people talked about making six figures or becoming millionaires. But today's financial bar is raised to a whole new level. Now we are talking about billions and trillions of dollars like it's nothing. Today's wealthy will be tomorrow's middle class.

Here is what the new financial bar looks like:

» The middle class are the new poor.
» Millionaires are becoming the new middle class.
» Billionaires are the new rich.
» Trillionaires are the new elite.

The bar has been raised, but most people have not upgraded their financial targets. They are stuck in the dream of becoming middle class earners or millionaires. The middle class will tell you that they feel poor, and today's millionaires will say that they don't feel wealthy. In fact, many of them are squeezed financially. You need to become a decamillionaire at the very least. It is the only way to meet any decent standard of living when you get older.

Press the Reset Button

Every time you reach the next financial level, you must reset your mind. To jump from $100K to $1 million, or from $1 million to $10 million, or from $10 million to $1 billion, you have to change the way you think and work. As my coach on the Atlanta Motor Speedway said, "Forget everything you know about driving slow."

To see dollars in the millions or billions, you must reset your imagination. Whatever becomes "seeable" becomes believable, and what is believable becomes possible. Write down your new financial target number every day. Memorize the number of zeros it has. Be able to write them out without hesitation. Become familiar. Then believe it is possible, and the "how to" will appear.

When I started to live out of my imagination, I realized that I had surrounded myself with people suffering from a common disease. It's called *possibility blindness*. They could not see what I saw: fields ripe for harvest, rivers of milk and honey, and opportunities all around me. All they saw were "giants"—not real giants but roadblocks and the sacrifices my dream required. I had learned to see pink elephants in Africa and golf clubs that I could own. They couldn't see any of that. Therefore, they couldn't understand why my standards were so high.

When the Israelites spied out the Promised Land, all but two of the spies became obsessed with the giants living there. The frightened spies said, "We were like grasshoppers in our own sight, and so we were in [the giants'] sight" (Numbers 13:33).

When I started to see my life the way the two faithful spies saw the Promised Land, the "grasshoppers" around me acted up. They wanted me to be a grasshopper too. When I refused, my grasshopper friends became my critics. They tried to convince me that I was crazy. They talked behind my back. They pressed me to settle for an average life of unfulfilled dreams and endless heartache.

Today, they want me to pay the bill at expensive restaurants.

‖‖‖‖‖‖‖‖‖‖‖‖‖‖‖‖‖‖‖‖ **FINANCIAL FAST TRACK FACT** ‖‖‖‖‖‖‖‖‖‖‖‖‖‖‖‖‖‖‖‖‖‖‖‖

YOU ARE NOT CRAZY FOR WANTING MORE OUT OF LIFE. YOU CAN HAVE IT ALL. YOU DESERVE MORE!

To keep moving forward, I had to tell myself the hard-core truth. I remember the pivotal moment when I said, "Yes! I want the very best that life can offer!"

Saying that was a game changer, but all I really did was tell myself the truth. I stopped hiding my desires behind piles of restrictive garbage and the shame that society and religion dump on people who want more.

Once I believed that I deserved more, I felt empowered to do more. That is when my opportunities for increase multiplied. Now I can help more people, the way I always wanted to. It was not an easy place to reach. I had to repeatedly tell myself, *I deserve a better life. I am worthy. I live in an abundant world full of resources. I deserve it.* Hit your reset button and keep pressing.

Which Way Is Higher?

En route to your promised land, it can be hard to know whose map is right and whose is wrong. One expert says we can't afford anything; we should live below our means and want nothing. The next says we need to stretch ourselves and find motivation by living above our means. The confusion keeps lots of people walking in circles.

I hope to untangle it by describing the five most common financial mindsets and their corresponding results. Within them, are some ideas you might not have considered before. Remember, this is the time to keep an open mind and consider other approaches to life and money.

Here are the five mindsets and the outcomes they produce:

1) Live above your means (bad stewardship leading to bankruptcy).
2) Live below your means (or "lower your means," deny your wants, and live in misery today).

3) Live at your means (stay on the treadmill, leading to stress and exhaustion).

4) Maximize your means (reduce your number one expense—taxes).

5) Lift your means (use your imagination to create more income for a better lifestyle).

You can live *above*, *below*, or *at* your means. Most middle-class people do one of the three. You can also *maximize* your means by reducing your expenditures, particularly your tax bill. That is something you should do, in any case. The fifth option, which few people ever talk about, is to let your imagination find ways of lifting your means to new heights.

When I looked at these five choices, I asked, "Which way of living is *higher*? Which one will stretch my faith? Which will force me to grow as a person? Which will get me to the top the soonest?"

I chose to *lift* my means, so I could live the lifestyle I really wanted. That meant using my imagination to increase my cash flow and become a millionaire. In other words, I owned my desire for an abundant life.

My friend, instead of shrinking your expectations, I am challenging you to dream your way to wealth and expand your future financial possibilities. Don't live below your potential. Lift your standards, expectations, means, and faith higher. Reach for the abundant life.

FINANCIAL FAST TRACK FACT

NOTHING CHANGES IN YOUR LIFE UNTIL YOU LIFT YOUR EXPECTATIONS.

I'm not advocating insanity. A fifth grader knows that if you spend more than you make, you will go broke. The deeper issue is *why* people do that in the first place. I believe it's because they want to live better than what they can afford.

Wanting the nicer things in life is not wrong; it is a natural desire. God put the first man in paradise, which was full of nice things, He allowed the man and his eventual family to have all of it except for one tree. God is generous toward us. He takes pleasure in our achievements and wants us to enjoy what life has to offer (Joshua 1:15; Psalms 35:27; Ecclesiastes 3:13; 1 Timothy 6:17).

There is no pain or poverty in heaven. If you feel the need to suffer, drop it! Embrace the abundant life that was meant to be. Jesus suffered, so you don't have to. He became sick, so you don't have to be sick. He also became poor—one time on the cross—so you don't have to be poor anymore (2 Corinthians 8:9).

Why do we overthink and over-spiritualize everything? Why do we use the club of "living below your means" to kill someone else's faith, dreams, and desires? Telling people to live below their means takes the wind out of their sails. It's almost inhumane, especially to those who are wired for entrepreneurship. Relegating them to their "now" realities instead of what they imagine for their future causes possibility blindness and denies their place as God's image bearers.

‖‖‖‖‖‖‖‖‖‖‖‖‖‖‖‖‖‖‖‖‖ **FINANCIAL FAST TRACK FACT** ‖‖‖‖‖‖‖‖‖‖‖‖‖‖‖‖‖‖‖‖‖

LIVING ABOVE YOUR MEANS ISN'T YOUR GREATEST OBSTACLE. LIVING BELOW YOUR POTENTIAL IS.

You cannot sentence people to settling for dreamless lives and then expect them to be enthusiastic about changing their financial situations. They need permission. They need affirmation. They need to be reminded that God wants each of them to live in their promised land.

Many people resist this idea. I understand where the resistance comes from, but it's toxic. Some have accused me of being "all about prosperity" because they don't understand that the message is not about money. It's about our potential. When we maximize that, prosperity is inevitable.

The Ocean of Abundance—Millions, Billions, and Trillions

I have asked you to consider ideas about money that might seem foreign. It might be difficult to wrap your head around the financial figures I listed. Any hesitancy you feel reveals your allegiance to a framework of scarcity rather than abundance.

Let me help you cross over. Imagine that you are standing on the Atlantic shoreline with wave upon wave upon wave crashing at your feet. If you believe that after each wave, another will come, you can begin to understand the abundance that is working all around you.

Now imagine that you want to draw water from the ocean. You can draw it out with a teaspoon or with trash cans filled to the brim. Even if you filled up an oil tanker with sea water, the ocean wouldn't flinch or be affected. You can take as much as you want, and you will not exhaust the supply.

It's like that with the sun. Can you absorb all the sun's rays? Does the sunlight hitting your face detract from someone else's portion? Absolutely not! There is enough for everyone to enjoy simultaneously. And that sun will keep rising and shining, day after day.

I could go on and on. There's enough oxygen for everyone and enough soil to cover the whole earth. The earth produces enough seeds to keep the harvests coming. The earth displays God's abundance because He created it that way. The only shortage is in our minds.

> *I have come that they might have life . . . more abundantly.*
> —JESUS CHRIST (JOHN 10:10)

> *Out of abundance they took abundance, and still abundance remained.*[26]
> —THE UPANISHADS

There is no shortage of money either. An infinite supply awaits those who apply the principles of acquiring it. Do not believe the lie of lack. Wealth is a renewable resource. When you have abundance, you have no issues with earning, giving, and sharing. You have plenty, and you know that behind every dollar, there is another and another and another.

There is an asteroid called 16 Psyche. It is 140 miles in diameter and orbits between 235 million and 309 million miles around the sun.[27] It is comprised mostly of iron and nickel, with traces of gold, copper, tungsten, and other elements.[28] From what scientists know about 16 Psyche, it would have a market value of $10,000 quadrillion, or $10,000,000,000,000,000,000.

---

26 Paul, "Abundance Gratitude," *The Gratitude Blog*, 16 Apr. 2010, https://allaboutgratitude.com/898/abundance-gratitude/.

27 "16 Psyche," *NASA*, accessed September 20, 2021, https://solarsystem.nasa.gov/asteroids-comets-and-meteors/asteroids/16-psyche/in-depth/.

28 Patrick J. Kiger, "Why Is an Asteroid Worth $10,000, 000, 000, 000, 000, 000?" *How Stuff Works*, 5 Nov. 2020, https://science.howstuffworks.com/psyche-16-asteroid.htm.

Do all those zeros make your eyes cross? The number dwarfs the 2020 combined global GDP of $84.54 trillion.[29] It is enough to give every man, woman, and child on Planet Earth more than a billion dollars.

If you focus on abundance, you will see abundance. When you focus on lack, you will always find it. The Law of Concentration says that whatever you focus on becomes magnified.[30] This can work for you or against you, depending on whether you are thinking in terms of increase or decrease.

Go ahead. Choose.

Shrinking Thinking Destroys Your Motivation

Is your imagination expanding or contracting? If it's contracting, you will naturally move toward lack and away from the motivation to do great things. But if you focus on lifting, expansion, and increase, you will move toward abundance.

Your future financial well-being depends on your approach. Lowering your means and expectations is the first sign that you are infected with possibility blindness and the diminished inner fire that accompanies it. You are using your imagination to create decrease when you could be igniting your passion for new and creative ways to elevate your means.

When I say the words "lower your means," how do you feel? What happens to your energy level? Does it drop?

Exactly! Remember: money is attracted to high energy, not low energy.

Here's what I mean: Imagine that you are overweight and your prescription for reducing is to starve yourself for forty years. Does that plan energize you? Do you feel excited about tackling weight loss?

Of course not!

The same is true about money. Shrinking thinking creates poverty living. There is nothing motivating or energizing about living in the prison of self-denial, especially for extended periods of time. That is, unless being a "rich" miser is your definition of success. In that case, this book isn't for you.

Sure, you can lower your standards and live below your means. You could even live in a nice, cheap, roach- and rat-infested apartment. Maybe eat rice and beans every night. Get your wardrobe at Goodwill and garage sales. Fly coach in the cheap middle seat with two screaming kids on each side of you. Drive an old beater

---

29 Aaron O'Neill, "Global Gross Domestic Product (GDP) at Current Prices from 1985 to 2026, *Statista*, 30 July 2021, https://www.statista.com/statistics/268750/global-gross-domestic-product-gdp/.

30 "Law of Concentration: What Is?" *MasterMind Matrix*, 28 Dec. 2015, https://mastermindmatrix.com/knowledge-base/law-of-concentration/.

that needs a quart of oil every week. Give up movie date nights and skip the freshly popped popcorn.

Do you honestly think that people who live that way are happy? I don't. But they could be lying to themselves. I did it for years.

||||||||||||||||||||||||||||| **FINANCIAL FAST TRACK FACT** |||||||||||||||||||||||||||||||||||

IF YOU'RE GOING TO QUIT SOMETHING, QUIT TRYING TO GO LOWER IN ORDER TO MOVE HIGHER.

When I was younger, one of my millionaire mentors gave me some correction. I was complaining about inflation and rising gas prices. He said, "Son, things aren't too expensive. You just can't afford them, and at your age, that's a real problem."

He was right. When I tried the shrinking-thinking-scarcity path for a couple of months, I felt like I needed antidepressants. I was miserable, and so was my wife. She really enjoyed our date nights, and I really enjoyed how those evenings ended. But now we were demotivated, with no joy, no sex, and a debt mountain that looked like Everest.

The day my life changed was the day I (1) started using my imagination to create the bigger and better future I really wanted, (2) started using my faith to move mountains of bad debt and financial lack out of my way, and (3) stopped using the scarcity strategy of living a cheap life.

Ready to move some mountains? Good! Here are some mountain-moving faith points to keep in mind:

» It takes no faith to shrink back (Hebrews10:35–36).

» It takes no faith to lower your means.

» It takes no faith to be a minimalist (homeless people achieve that).

» It takes no faith to deny your wants and needs.

You have to move up to another level of thinking, which is true for me and everybody else. Everybody has to learn to think differently; bigger, to be open to possibilities.[31]
—OPRAH WINFREY, FIRST BLACK FEMALE BILLIONAIRE

Before we go any further, I want to challenge any possibility blindness that may be restricting your vision to the here and now and suppressing the power of your infinite imagination. When you can see what *is* but not what *could be*, you are blind to possibility.

Get out of your comfort zone and decide to live an expanded lifestyle. An abundant future awaits you. Get out of your head, and start living in the greatness of your imagination. Take the advice of my past mentor, and *live in the future today.*

---

31 Glenn Van Ekeren, "Are You the Lid?" *Linked In*, 27 June 2019, https://www.linkedin.com/pulse/you-lid-glenn-van-ekeren?trk=related_artice_Are%20You%20The%20Lid%3F_article-card_title.

. . . .

FINANCIAL FAST TRACK COACHING

Practice imagining an abundant lifestyle. See yourself living in the home of your dreams, enjoying ideal relationships, and contributing to the world through your unique talents and abilities. Imagine the fortune you could create and the good it could do.

See it. Believe it. What is seeable becomes believable. What is believable becomes possible!

1) It's time to use your imagination and travel into your future—now!

What do you see in the future?

Who are you?

What are you doing?

How much money do you have?

How many people are you helping?

2) It's time to make some choices.

Do you want Level 1 and Level 2 wealth, or will you set new financial targets at Level 3 and beyond?

Why or why not?

3) Warning! Not making a choice is a choice. Set your desired wealth number (the number of days you can choose not to work without having to change your lifestyle).

My new wealth number is _____.

4) In what ways has possibility blindness kept you from believing you could be more, do more, or have more?

3

IMAGE**A**CTION

When you make your living speaking in front of crowds, a global pandemic is a serious blow. Travel ceases, and government shutdowns mean venues are closed anyway. Then staffers discover that unemployment is more profitable than working, so they jump ship.

That's where I found myself in 2020. After twenty-five-plus years of speaking, coaching, and training leaders around the world, I stood in my garage with computers, paperwork, and product inventory stacked around me. There were only two ways to respond: I could sit down, shut up, and believe the lie that says, "I have done it all. Why do it again?" or I could push back and reframe my dream.

Either way, I had to ask God whether the Confidence Coaching brand was over. As tears ran down my face, a Bible story came to mind about four lepers who faced a pandemic and famine (2 Kings 7:1–8). They were marginalized, rejected, and shunned by just about everyone. They were sick, homeless, and hungry too.

It doesn't get much worse than that (unless they were also ugly). But amid a worst-case scenario, what I call *imagineAction* kicked in. One leper used it to create a plan for new possibilities and a better life. He encouraged the others, saying, "What are we going to do, just sit here until we die?"

He realized that sitting meant death was guaranteed. But if they could imagine a better outcome and take action, they had at least a fifty-fifty chance of surviving. So, the lepers went into action and raided the enemy camp! It was a bold call, and it paid off. They came out with riches—silver, gold, and fancy clothing. Instead of being victims with no hope, they became heroes in their own story—all through the power of *imagineAction*!

As I remembered their story, hope came alive- in my heart. I wiped my tears and remembered my 2002 trip to the bottom of the barrel. It was a similar situation, and God brought me out. ImagineAction was all I had back then, so I imagined a new future and committed to taking massive action to get there. My goals were ambitious: I would speak in front of a crowd every day of the year, and I would speak to one million people in my lifetime.

Most of my critics laughed and said those things would never happen. My goals *were* audacious, and I didn't know whether they were achievable or not. But I learned that most people never imagine anything big enough to be life-changing. I knew that if my dream couldn't transform where I lived, what I drove, where I shopped, and whom I hung around, it wasn't big or high enough to motivate consistent, massive action.

FINANCIAL FAST TRACK FACT

THE NUMBER ONE REASON PEOPLE DON'T ACHIEVE THEIR GOALS IS BECAUSE THEY DON'T IMAGINE ANYTHING BIG AND HIGH ENOUGH TO CHANGE THEIR LIVES.

So I aimed big and high, which took me into a season of what I call *deliberate extreme*. It's a decision most people never make, but it is necessary for radical change.

Bonnie and I talked it over and agreed that creating financial success was going to cost us something. We decided that I would make the money, and she would manage it. I would cold call for speaking opportunities from 8:00 a.m. until 5:00 p.m., for a minimum of fifty calls each day. (I teach my students an easier plan today.) When my cold-calling was done, we would eat dinner together. Then I would return to my office and work on my confidence book from 9:00 p.m. until 3:00 a.m. A twelve-pack of Diet Coke helped me grind out the pages each night.

> *Imagination is everything. It is a preview of life's coming attractions.*[32]
> —ALBERT EINSTEIN

Do It Now

Earlier we saw the importance of thinking like a king, which means thinking on a higher plane—*really* higher. Kings also think fast. They want things done now, or yesterday, if possible. King Darius is a great example. The Bible reveals how he thought and worked. When he wanted the temple to be restored, he declared, "I Darius issue a decree; let it be done with speed" (Ezra 6:12, KJV).

〜〜〜〜〜〜〜 **FINANCIAL FAST TRACK FACT** 〜〜〜〜〜〜〜

PROCRASTINATION IS THE LOVER OF THE NONACHIEVER.

When I decided my life had to change, I applied a king's principles. There was no lag time between what I saw in my imagination and when I got to work. Slow success is no success. I didn't put up a "dream board" or write down the vision and say, "Wow. Someday. . . ." Someday isn't a day of the week; it's just another word for *never*. I had to act on my imagination immediately. That was my mantra, and it needs to be yours.

I accomplished what my imagineAction prescribed! According to my wife, I traveled for speaking engagements 325 days out of 365 by 2016. The only thing that stopped me from meeting my goal was a heart attack on December 7, the day of our twenty-five-year anniversary. (My wife jokes that I was trying to get out of going on a nice dinner date.) But watch this: at some destinations,

---

32 Liz Shanks, "Imagination Is Everything. It Is the Preview of Life's Coming Attractions," *Liz's Book Snuggery*, 11 Aug. 2019, http://www.lizsbooksnuggery.com/2019/08/einstein-imagination-everything-preview-lifes-coming-attractions/.

I spoke in several places on the same day. Technically, I exceeded my goal, and that was without the help of today's more advanced social media.

Fast-forward to my garage in 2020. I decided not to be a victim of the pandemic. Instead, I would become the hero of my own story. If the lepers could do it, so could I. I wasn't going to succumb to the circumstances, even if other people had no choice.

It's important to mention the people who were not forced to surrender but quit anyway. As I write, companies are offering sign-on bonuses to attract unskilled and other workers who have not returned to work. Jobs await them, but they're not biting. I believe they are burned out from years of barely getting by. The stress of that is exhausting! During the COVID shutdowns, something dawned on them: the payoff for their employment isn't enough to get them off the couch and back onto the hamster wheel.

I'm not advocating a lifetime without work. That is not a healthy prospect. But I am acknowledging what millions are feeling. Burnout is keeping them on the sidelines.

So, what's the cure for burnout? It's a massive payoff. If I offered you a dollar to detail my car in the hot Florida sun, would you drive an hour each way to do it? Probably not because the payoff is too low. Why would you burn yourself out for a buck? But if I offered you $1 million dollars for the gig, your motivation would return, and fast.

When COVID messed with my business model, I still had a payoff worth fighting for. I immediately activated an imagineAction strategy: I would immediately change my business model, so flying was not necessary. And guess what? The new model worked! While the business world panicked over the pandemic, I had a record year. Instead of getting left behind, I leapt ahead.

FINANCIAL FAST TRACK FACT

ACTION OPENS THE DOOR TO OPPORTUNITY.

I won't kid you. The road less traveled will get you some nasty press. Back when I first realized how my imagination could shape my finances, I eagerly shared the news with my pastor friends. I knew some of their struggles and honestly thought that what I learned would be game-changing for them.

They didn't see it that way. Instead, they made fun and gossiped about my being theologically off base. They saw no value in having a larger vision, and guess what? They are still pastoring the same small churches, and some are even smaller now. They are living on the same salaries, driving the same cars, and living in the same tiny houses as they did fifteen-plus years ago. Nothing changed.

Meanwhile, I have been granted greater influence, impact, and income. I have more to give, more ways to help, and more opportunities to use whatever gifts and talents God has given me.

If you ask my old pastor friends why they're still in the same place, they'll recite a laundry list of reasons: "It's the devil." "It's the Christians in the area." "It's the church's location." They have even convinced themselves that they are called to stay small and are having an impact.

Please understand that "big" and "wealthy" are not the only measures of success. What I'm questioning are the ways we justify what isn't working. None of these pastors ever told me, "Man, it's great! I have been imagining, asking, and planning for small, and it's working." Nor have they said, "I'm not getting anywhere because I'm too lazy to take massive action."

I get where they're coming from. I was there once and had to ask myself some hard-hitting questions that I continue to ask myself. We all need to answer them at some point:

What has been the high cost of my own inaction?

What relationships have I lost?

How much money have I lost?

How many opportunities have passed me by?

How much self-inflicted pain and stress has this caused me?

Remember, all "imagineers" and massive action-takers were laughed at before they rose to the top. Don't let that worry you. Your imagination is your thought factory. It produces fifty thousand thoughts per day, including some that can create millions, billions, or trillions of dollars. Ask Amazon founder Jeff Bezos, who is on course to become a trillionaire. Or ask Elon Musk, who is planning for humans to colonize Mars. A single million- or billion-dollar idea that is acted upon has the power to change the entire world and shape our reality. These dreamers are proving it!

▓▓▓▓▓▓▓▓▓▓▓▓▓▓▓▓ **FINANCIAL FAST TRACK FACT** ▓▓▓▓▓▓▓▓▓▓▓▓▓▓▓▓▓

YOUR THOUGHTS, IDEAS, AND ACTIONS CONTROL WHERE, HOW FAST, AND HOW FAR YOU GO IN LIFE.

Don't Think Fast, Think Facebook Fast

After hacking Harvard's student directory to create FaceMash (a Harvard-only version of Hot or Not in 2003),[33] Mark Zuckerberg caught the attention of twin brothers Tyler and Cameron Winklevoss and their classmate, Divya Narendra. The trio shared an idea with Zuckerberg called HarvardConnection,[34] an online networking platform for students.

Zuckerberg envisioned something much bigger. Using the university as a beta-test, he created "the facebook thing" within weeks.[35] Today, Facebook is a social-media juggernaut that recently crossed the $1 trillion mark.[36] In 2020, Zuckerberg had an estimated net worth of $127 billion.[37] Not bad for a guy in his thirties.

What accounts for Zuckerberg's success? He used his imagineAction to think bigger and act even faster. Had he not done both, he might have ended up a HarvardConnection employee. Instead, what his imagination created drove him, and he acted with urgency.

Your God-like creative abilities will produce your desired financial abundance. Your infinite imagination will birth new, wealth-building strategies. If you allow small people to limit your big thoughts, they will destroy your creativity and derail your destiny.

33 Alexia Tsotsis, "Facemash.com, Home of Zuckerberg's Facebook Predecessor, For Sale," *TechCrunch*, 5 Oct. 2010, https://techcrunch.com/2010/10/05/facemash-sale/.

34 Ben Mezrich, "'He Thinks We're Going to Take a Swing at Him?' Inside the Decades-Long Cage Match Between Mark Zuckerberg and the Winklevoss Twins," *Vanity Fair*, 30 Apr. 2019, https://www.vanityfair.com/news/2019/04/inside-the-mark-zuckerberg-winklevoss-twins-cage-match.

35 Nicholas Carlson, "At Last—the Full Story of How Facebook Was Founded," *Business Insider*, 5 March 2010, https://www.businessinsider.com/how-facebook-was-founded-2010-3.

36 Shalini Nagarajan, "Facebook Is Now Worth $1 Trillion after a US Court's Dismissal of 2 Antitrust Lawsuit Spurs Jump in Stock," *Business Insider*, 29 June 2021, https://markets.businessinsider.com/news/stocks/facebook-market-cap-1-trillion-antitrust-lawsuit-dismissal-judge-monopoly-2021-6.

37 Kenrick Cai, "Mark Zuckerberg Has Sold Facebook Stock Almost Every Weekday This Year," *Forbes*, 13 July 2021, https://www.forbes.com/sites/kenrickcai/2021/07/13/mark-zuckerberg-has-sold-facebook-stock-almost-every-weekday-this-year/?sh=6aeaeb4269d4.

The formula is simple: **ideas + inspiration = divine possibilities**. You cannot create and produce beyond what you can imagine. Even your finances cannot exceed the capacity of your imagination. Yet, even with no money in your pocket, you can imagine big things and act quickly. You can create solutions for significant problems. That is your financial accelerator. Punch it!

One good idea can mean living like a king for life.

FINANCIAL FAST TRACK FACT

GOD WILL "SHOW YOU GREAT AND MIGHTY THINGS." —JEREMIAH 33:3 HE KNOWS WHERE THE GOLD IS. ONE IDEA FROM HIM CAN CHANGE YOUR FINANCIAL FUTURE.

Beyond Positive Thinking

I believe in the power of positive thinking. But without positive actions, you will positively produce no results. Multimillionaires and billionaires are *action-aires*. Acting on what they imagined got them where they are today.

The personal development movement encouraged people to read more books. I'm all for reading; it's a resource for discovering and igniting great ideas. I coached one guy who read over three hundred books but never took the first step toward building his business. Another leader I coached jumped on airplanes and attended two seminars each month. His credit cards funded his addiction to learning. Ideas that he could have taken to the bank drove him into bankruptcy instead.

Remember: persistent action produces prosperity; passivity causes poverty.

FINANCIAL FAST TRACK FACT

READING ISN'T ACHIEVING, AND CONSUMING ISN'T PRODUCING.

Reading books, attending seminars, downloading podcasts, and watching YouTube tutorials are not substitutes for action. Gathering knowledge is important, but knowledge that is not acted upon is wasted. The same can be said about positive affirmations. Confession without action is delusion.

Do you ever wonder how someone can inhale all that stuff and still be broke? It's because consuming is *easy*. Anyone can hide in a recliner and bury their nose in a book. And anyone can hide in a church or conference room taking seminar after seminar.

Taking massive *action* is what separates winners from losers. It's like the balance between eating right and exercising. Eating steak is the fun part. But few are willing to load up the squat rack and convert that protein into muscle.

|||||||||||||||||||||||||||| **FINANCIAL FAST TRACK FACT** ||||||||||||||||||||||||||||

ACTION SEPARATES CONTENDERS FROM PRETENDERS.

Big, bold, fast action produces quick and powerful results. Knowledge is nothing more than potential power until someone has the guts to act on it. Procrastination is a parasite that sucks the life out of your dreams. Refuse to languish over your ideas and beliefs. Either act on them immediately, or resign yourself to mediocrity.

Mediocre and *average* were never part of God's plan for you. How you see your future determines the intensity of your emotional state. Your emotions will set you *in motion* and determine the size of the actions you will take. If you see a small future, you will feel unmotivated and take minimal actions, doing only what is required and producing just enough to survive.

If you envision a future filled with success, happiness, and prosperity, you are generating empowering, energy-producing emotions. Only they can trigger the massive action you need to get the "golf club" instead of the "putter." Success requires maximum effort that far exceeds what survival requires. This approach is the difference between an *almost* life and getting the *most* out of life.

Small thinkers don't get the big breaks. If you want to get richer, think bigger first.[38]
—Robert Kiyosaki, Best-selling Author

Three Success Levels

This is the Information Age, but information is not enough. Outrageous success requires outrageous actions. The questions are (1) whether you are acting or just dreaming, and (2) whether your actions are as outrageous as your dream.

According to Newton's Third Law of Motion, every action has an equal and opposite reaction. But there are levels of action and corresponding levels of success. If you pair big dreams with small actions, you contradict your desires. Where do you suppose that ends up?

John Maxwell has taught about three levels of success.[39] Let's look at them and the kind of action each demands:

» Level 1: Survival requires minimal effort, doing only what is necessary (living to get by).
» Level 2: Success requires great effort, beyond what is necessary (living to get ahead).
» Level 3: Significance requires maximum effort and raising the standard (living to leave a legacy).

Most people exert minimal effort and never become the people they are supposed to be. Some others exert great effort in becoming better versions of themselves and experience a degree of success. Very few people give their maximum effort to experience the joy of making a significant difference in the world (and a lot of money).

Minimum-effort people will always criticize those who give 100 percent. None of my super-successful mentors has ever told me to slow down and do less. It's always the small doers who say, "You work too hard. You're too busy."

I answer, "Compared to what?" But what I'm really thinking is, "Only compared to your lazy butt!"

Something else irks me. People who do as little as possible like the adage: "Good things come to those who wait." It's a bumper sticker for survival mode. I prefer saying, "Great things come to those who make them happen." Stop waiting for your ship to come in. Jump in the water and swim to it. It's the only way to create abundance and significance.

---

38 Robert T. Kiyosaki, *Rich Dad Poor Dad: What the Rich Teach Their Kids About Money—That the Poor and Middle Class Do Not!* (Lulu.com, 2019), 186.

39 John Maxwell taught these levels at a live seminar for the John Maxwell Coaching Team in Miami some years ago.

In the Spielberg classic *Catch Me If You Can*, Christopher Walken's character, Frank Abagnale Sr., tells a story while accepting an award from the Rotary Club:

Two little mice fell in a bucket of cream. The first mouse quickly gave up and drowned. The second mouse wouldn't quit. He struggled so hard that eventually he churned that cream into butter and crawled out. Gentlemen, as of this moment, I am that second mouse.[40]

Each mouse's result was commensurate with its effort. The second mouse knew nothing about making butter but fought valiantly to stay alive. Its effort solved its immediate problem and created something in the process.

Here's the lesson: **abundant changes = abundant opportunities = abundant money possibilities**. If you miss that, you'll never see the wealth you have worked for all your life. Remember that we are living in unprecedented, accelerated times. Change happens fast, but wherever it happens, opportunity shows up. All you need is one opportunity to live like a king.

But opportunities move fast too. In times like these, acting *now* is your secret to every financial windfall. Indecision is costly. I have seen spiritual people waste time praying about opportunities only to miss the moment. Often, God is speaking in the opportunity. Stop praying long enough to seize what is right in front of you!

Understand the Times

Nobody wants to live in the past, but many people do. If you understand the times in which you live but act on outdated formulas, you can work 'til you drop and die poor. The financial success formula for our times is **imagination + action x speed = fast financial results.**

Fast is the new *big*. Companies used to build for size. Now they build for speed. Culture is accelerating, and speed is what it demands. The only way to get rich is to do it fast. Getting rich quick is not a fantasy. If you don't get rich quickly, you might never get the chance at all. And if you are in the age group that can't wait another twenty to forty years, you know that's true.

This is not the Agricultural Age. You're not limited by acreage, crop yield, weather, and harvest season. You don't earn all your money once each year and hope it lasts 'til the next harvest. You're not limited to Industrial Age rules either. You don't have to be financially bound by the number of hours you can work or the amount of overtime you can get.

---

40 "Catch Me If You Can" (2002): Christopher Walken; Frank Abagnale," *IMDB*, accessed September 21, 2021, https://www.imdb.com/title/tt0264464/characters/nm0000686.

The world is different now. The Information Age has dissolved those limitations. Now speed is both your greatest obstacle and greatest opportunity. If you want to get rich, quick is the only method. I know, I know. You have been conditioned to believe that getting rich is evil and getting rich quickly is impossible. The culture has crammed the "slow boat to China" idea down your throat, and it's stuck there.

I'll say it again: it's a lie. The old-school teachers are not factoring in the current rate of change. In this climate, it is easier to get rich quickly than to follow the "wheelchair wealth" philosophy. In today's environment, to move slowly is to violate a core value of the culture, which is speed!

Let me share a secret. I promise it will be offensive, but if you will hear me out—and I mean *really* hear—you will consider the implications and change your life.

Culture trumps anointing. Culture even trumps the Word of God. Before you stone me, please remember that Jesus couldn't perform miracles where the culture's traditional ways of thinking prevented people from believing (Mark 6:4–6). When the culture prizes a particular value, it dictates what society will believe, do, or have.

In 2021, safe, slow, and steady are *out.* People no longer have the time or tolerance to build wealth later. It's now or never.

Listen, faith thinking is *now* thinking (Hebrews 11:1). God thinks and acts higher and faster. Through His imagination, He created the universe in six days. That is what I call *fast.* Science is still trying to figure it out!

You are not the Almighty, but you can create a better life. Will you commit to taking big, bold leaps instead of little baby steps? I know that's not how you were trained. None of us were. You must reprogram yourself to make faster decisions. Make it a discipline. If you practice it, you will have a greater chance of success now than in any time in history.

Four Levels of Value

Are you wondering, How do I do it faster? Your question is valid. Although we have exited the Agricultural and Industrial Ages, you might still feel limited in your capacity to earn. The challenge lies in four levels of value, particularly if you are operating in the wrong one. Myron Golden shared this concept with me years ago, from his "Make More Offers" seminar.[41]

41 Shared here with permission.

Study the four levels of the Value Mountain and identify (1) where you are now and (2) where you need to be for building real wealth.

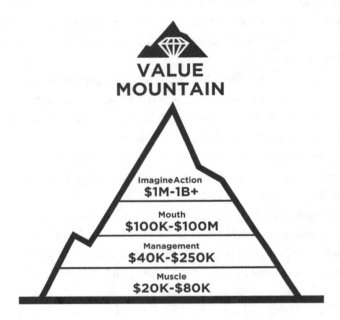

Muscle Level

The *muscle level* typically involves physical labor but includes other positions in an organization's work force. The harder and longer you push your body, the more you earn. Increase comes from increased hourly pay, fitting more jobs into your workday, or working longer hours. Whether you hold a blue- or white-collar position, your opportunity to earn more is limited. Muscle-level earners are typically capped at around $80,000 a year.

Management Level

Management is responsible for what muscle-level workers produce. In exchange for that responsibility, managers receive higher salaries. However, they bear responsibility for productivity and work insane hours to keep things running smoothly. People who fulfill this role with professionalism can expect to earn between $40,000 and $250,000 a year.

Mouth Level

This is where things get interesting. Communication is one of the most important skills on the planet, which makes public speaking one of the highest-paid professions. Yes, speakers, YouTube marketers, and digital online course creators can make more than doctors, lawyers, and engineers. With the right message crafted for the right market and delivered through the right medium, you can earn anywhere from $100,000 to $100 million.

ImagineAction Level[42]

Your income is limited only by your imagination—truly. At the *imagination level*, one idea can change the world and your family's finances for generations. You are paid in direct proportion to the problems you solve. Solve bigger problems, and your income can soar anywhere from $1 million to $1 billion. Earners at this level will soon earn trillions. Elon Musk is a good example. He is using his imagination to create self-driving electric cars, robots, internet satellites, and rocket ships to colonize Mars. Like Jeff Bezos, Musk is expected to become one of the world's first modern-day trillionaires.[43]

||||||||||||||||||||||||||| **FINANCIAL FAST TRACK FACT** |||||||||||||||||||||||||||

SET A NEW IMAGINEACTION GOAL TO BECOME A MULTIMILLIONAIRE, NOT FOR THE MONEY BUT FOR THE PERSON YOU BECOME TO MAKE IT.

When you decide to move up from the muscle and management levels, your mouth and imagination will accelerate your financial success by quantum leaps. Remember: **imagination + action x speed = fast financial results**.

Friend, I urge you to think in terms of imagineAction, and do it now! W. Clement Stone was a success guru, founder of *Success Unlimited* magazine, and a philanthropist who gave over $275 million to charity. He had a success

---

42   Myron Golden calls this the "imagination" level. I call it *imagineAction*.

43   Minda Zetlin, "Here's Why Elon Musk Could Be the World's First Trillionaire, According to Billionaire VC," *Inc.*, accessed September 25, 2021, https://www.inc.com/minda-zetlin/elon-musk-trillionaire-tesla-shares-chamath-palihapitiya.html.

phrase that he believed was responsible for his wealth; the phrase was "Do it Now!"[44] He made himself and those who worked for him say it one hundred times each day.

Life is short. Whatever you want to do, be, have, and help, this is your time. Don't wait for tomorrow; it might never come. Don't wait for the storms and pandemics to clear. Take imagineAction in spite of them. You have everything to gain.

---

44 From an Eileen Wilder marketing piece distributed at a 2021 Click Funnels event.

· · · · · · · · · ·

FINANCIAL FAST TRACK COACHING

It's time to unmask negative beliefs! I often challenge my coaching clients to set their goals at becoming millionaires or (if they are already millionaires) decamillionaires. Money is great, but this goal is not about money or material possessions. It's about what I've already mentioned: the person you become in reaching that level.

Consider the following:

» The size of your thinking isn't enough. If it were, you would already be at your goal.

» If you're saying, "There's no way I could ever become a millionaire or a decamillionaire," your level of thinking has already been revealed. Work on changing it.

» You might say, "I don't have any negative belief systems." Yes, I know; I used to think that too. That is why I created the following exercises.

1) What is your current income? _____

Take the last digit from the number you just wrote down, and write it here: _____

Do you believe you can do something stupid enough to reduce your income to that second figure, in just one year? (Obviously, your answer is *yes*. Everyone can do something that stupid!)

2) Next, take your current income and add another zero at the end.

_____

This is your potential income for this year. How does that sound? Are you thinking, *This isn't possible*? If so, your excuses are trying to maintain control.

Maybe you haven't said it was impossible. Maybe you are saying, "Yes, but. . . ." Stop! List all your "Yes, buts" below (add as many lines as you need):

_____

_____

_____

_____

_____

_____

_____

_____

See, you had no problem believing you could reduce your income, but you struggled to imagine more. For all the reasons you just wrote down, you lacked the confidence to add that zero.

All—and I emphasize, *all*—of the "buts" you listed are lies you tell yourself to keep from taking responsibility for generating wealth.

Yes. You are lying to yourself. The lies about not multiplying your income by a factor of ten are the same lies that keep you from making an extra $5,000 or $10,000 a year. The stories and excuses playing in your head have put the brakes on your finances, year after year.

Is the "extra zero" number realistic? I don't know. But the point is to reveal the belief systems that are buried deep in your subconscious mind.

The mind, once stretched by a new idea, never returns to its
original dimensions.[45]
—RALPH WALDO EMERSON

45 "Ralph Waldo Emerson > Quotes > Quotable Quotes," *Goodreads*, accessed October 23, 2021, https://www.goodreads.com/quotes/37815-the-mind-once-stretched-by-a-new-idea-never-returns.

4

RELEASE THE EMERGENCY BRAKE

Money loves speed,[46] and friction slows it down. When you gun your financial engine, make sure you're not braking at the same time. If there's friction in your head, your plan, or your actions, root it out.

As a teenager, my second car was a Ford Galaxy convertible with a 390 engine. I loved that car. It had a four-speed manual transmission so powerful that I took extra precautions, even setting the emergency brake when I parked the thing.

Waking up late for school one day, I jumped in the car and took off, but just barely. I couldn't accelerate above 15 mph and had the horrible thought that my engine was shot. It took forever to go ten miles.

That morning, I lost confidence in the Ford Motor Company, the 390 engine, and the Galaxy model. I punched the steering wheel and ranted, "This car is a piece of junk!"

Suddenly, smoke rose from my tires. I looked at the dash and noticed that my emergency brake light was on. I had driven all that way with the brake engaged!

My lack of speed wasn't Ford's fault, the engine's fault, or the car's fault. A stupid decision had slowed me down. Once I released the brake, my car was free to operate like a car with a 390 engine should.

---

46 Vitale, *Money Loves Speed!* xiii.

Could it be that you are driving your financial vehicle with your emergency brake on?

|||||||||||||||||||||||||||| **FINANCIAL FAST TRACK FACT** ||||||||||||||||||||||||||||

YOUR FINANCIAL FAST TRACK BEGINS WITH FINANCIAL CONFIDENCE, NOT FINANCIAL FREEDOM!

Check Your Goals

Financial freedom is a popular catchphrase and a widely accepted goal. Many financial gurus prescribe baby steps, strategies, and tactics to help you get there. However, financial freedom isn't the number one goal when fast-tracking your finances. Financial freedom is a moving target. You can reach it in one season and watch it crash the next.

I was invited to a private group coaching event with Jack Canfield, the coauthor of the famous *Chicken Soup for the Soul* book series. During our session, he flashed an image on the projector screen. It was the mansion he bought after selling more than 100 million copies of his first book.

Everyone in the room ooohed and aaahed.

Then Canfield asked, "Do you want to know the number one decision you will ever make concerning your future financial success? It's choosing whom you marry. Last week my divorce was finalized. I got to keep my mansion. She got all the money we had in the bank from my book sales and all the furniture in the house. Today, I am financially broke, but I know I can get it all back tomorrow."

Wow. The friction in his marriage slowed him down for a moment. It looked like he'd lost everything, but he didn't lose the one thing that would make a difference: he never lost his financial confidence or intellectual property.

Back in the 1980s, one of my celebrity clients had a multimillion-dollar television studio and $10 million in cash. After the news media turned against him, he lost everything. Like Jack Canfield, however, he held onto his financial confidence. Now, in his seventies, he still dreams of making a huge impact in this generation, and he has a list of achievements to fulfill before he turns eighty. As we speak, he's on a path to get back everything, and then some.

Financial Confidence and Drag

Financial confidence is the internal, absolute certainty that you can generate, multiply, and distribute money no matter what negative circumstances come your way. It is believing that you are not crazy for wanting to be more, do more, and have more. It goes beyond positive thinking. It is positively knowing that you're not too old or too young (or too anything) to have visions and dreams.

Your financial freedom and independence can be stripped away at any time. Divorce, a global pandemic, a stock market collapse, illness, shifting trends, government interference, false accusations, a stupid decision, a new competitor, a geographical change, a lawsuit, the news media, or the IRS can reverse your fortunes fast. However, the storms of life cannot strip away your financial confidence.

I love race cars. They are designed to be aerodynamic. A car with a huge engine but a shape like a refrigerator won't go fast. However, if you redesign it with minimal air-flow friction, you will minimize drag and maximize speed.

Now consider your speed on the Financial Fast Track. If you find a great vehicle but run it on outdated money beliefs, you will experience drag. Your ideas will slow you down and cause you to finish last. As Ricky Bobby said in *Talladega Nights*, "If you ain't first, you're last!"[47]

This chapter will help you identify the drag caused by limiting belief systems. You must identify them because they are destroying your financial confidence and preventing acceleration toward your financial dreams.

Confidence-Killing Financial "Brakes"

Everyone has belief systems that operate undetected. They are so automatic that you don't see them working against you. You just keep hitting the same plateaus and roadblocks and wondering why you're still stuck. Let's look at six of the most common "brakes," so we can disengage them.

1) **Entitlement thinking:** The government, my parents, and society owe me something for nothing. This thought process cripples belief in your own brilliance and ability to use your mind, skills, and talents to build a financial fortress and become a contributor instead of a taker.

2) **Scarcity thinking:** My resources are limited, so I better save, hoard, and live the poor life of a miserable miser. You can get debt free, live in a mansion, become a billionaire, and still have a scarcity mindset. "Poor" thinking attacks all classes.

---

47 "If You Ain't First, You're Last," *YouTube*, posted by CineClips, 2 May 2020, https://www.youtube.com/watch?v=ar1McsRmBOk.

3) **Minimalist thinking:** I don't need worldly possessions to be happy. So, let's see how small I can live while pretending I am happy in my tiny house and little car. If you need to prove that you can handle deprivation, you are focused on the wrong things.

4) **Victim thinking:** Rich villains are taking advantage of me. Therefore, I can do nothing to get ahead. I guess I will remain poor until I get to heaven. This mindset not only keeps you hog-tied but keeps you shifting blame for circumstances you have the power to change.

5) **"No" thinking:** I'm so used to "no" that it's hard to think "yes." I've heard it said that by the age of eighteen, most people are conditioned by having heard no tens of thousands of times. When opportunity comes, the ingrained no keeps them from seizing the moment and taking action. No is the brake on your vehicle. Yes is your financial accelerator.

6) **Religious thinking:** Money is the root of all evil. It will destroy my relationship with God, cause me to be and do evil things, and is totally unspiritual. By "religious thinking," I mean ideas that sound pious but distort the truth. Scripture says that "the love of money (better translated as lust) is a root of all kinds of evil" (1 Timothy 6:10).

While studying for my doctorate, I discovered that nearly all frictional beliefs about money have been spread through religious institutions. It doesn't matter whether you are religious or not; these beliefs have restricted you. It is important to know where they came from because destroying them will remove dream-killing drag.

I've already alluded to the number one "religious emergency brake," which is misunderstanding the Bible. Your interpretation of Scripture is either high-octane fuel in your race car or a fire hose extinguishing your burning desire to succeed. Sadly, many preachers pluck a couple of Bible verses and ignore their context. Until they learn to teach the whole story, they cannot empower anyone to make wise decisions.

The Bible is one of the best informational books on wisdom, success, and achievement ever written. Why? Because it describes people who won with money and people who lost with money. True wisdom is gained by studying successes *and* failures.

The Bible balances over a thousand positive promises on prosperity with warnings about wealth and poverty. If you're not careful, you can assume that Scripture contradicts itself. What it does is make comparisons. The following word lists describe some comparisons that Scripture makes:

BIBLE POSITIVES	BIBLE NEGATIVES
Right	Wrong
Success	Failure
Rich	Poor
Diligent	Lazy
Behold	Beware
Examples	Warnings
Happiness	Misery
Possibilities	Limitation
Abundance	Scarcity
Generosity	Stinginess
Ambition	Greed
Worker	Beggar
Wealth	Poverty

It is important to study both positive and negative stories to build true financial intelligence. However, many "spiritual" leaders and theologians are so concerned about your spiritual development that they neglect your financial intelligence. As a result, they minimize the positive words on the list and maximize the negative ones.

Yes! You can find examples of people who became rich only to crash and burn. You can also find people who allowed the stress and pressures of lack to destroy their walk with God and others. Every life has its own sources of friction.

Study the Victories and the Failures

The truth has been playing out through all of history, including Bible history. We need to read about how Adam and Eve failed by obsessing over one tree out of many. We also need the amazing stories of Abraham's faith and success as he continued to believe God's covenant of blessing.

It is important to read about how Job loved God, was a righteous man, and became the richest person in the East. We also need to understand that when fear caused him to lose everything, his story ended victoriously. God gave him double for everything he lost. At the same time, we must consider the parable of the rich young ruler who loved his money more than the opportunity to follow Jesus, the most influential man in world history (Luke 18:18–23). And don't forget the lazy man whose garden was overrun by thorns and weeds. We need to see how poverty overwhelmed him (Proverbs 24:30–34), so we don't repeat his mistakes.

On the other hand, we must study the disciples who gave everything to follow Jesus and then worked tirelessly to spread the gospel after His death, resurrection, and ascension. We need to remember that Jesus promised them as much as a hundredfold return on everything they left behind (Mark 10:29-30). We can also learn from the grievous example of Judas, who became history's biggest loser by selling out his values for thirty pieces of silver.

The most important story of all is about Jesus, the sinless man who selflessly laid down His life for the masses, so we could have eternal life, healing, and financial abundance.

FINANCIAL FAST TRACK QUESTION
IS YOUR MIND STUCK ON THE PERILS OF PROSPERITY?

Prosperity is complex, but we often reduce it to a *binary proposition.* On one side of the coin, we see peril. On the other, we see promise. But sandwiched between them is a third option, which is success. It comes from understanding the other two. This wisdom means you can learn from prosperity's perils and promises and approach them in a balanced manner.

THE
SUCCESS COIN

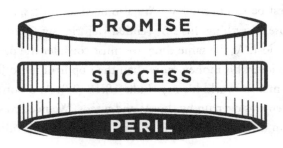

This balance is important because focusing only on the Bible's cautions will spawn fear, which puts the brakes on your financial potential. Please hear me: many wonderful and spiritual people are afraid to stretch their financial thinking because they misunderstand Scripture. They avoid getting rich because they fear what others will think of them if they do.

Many highly successful people have told me that they felt judged and intimidated when they came to church driving their luxury automobiles. I have heard megachurch leaders teach other megachurch leaders not to drive their "high-dollar" cars to church but hide them and their other "toys" at summer homes far from the church campus. In other words, having riches is not bad, but letting people see them is a problem. The solution? Live a fake middle-class life, so your congregation accepts you.

Do you hear the fear in that? Faith comes by hearing but so does fear. If year after year, you build a strong belief system that says you should be afraid of finances, money, success, and wealth, you will experience the consequences of that fear. This is the conditioning that many churches have promoted.

This book is about unlearning what you thought was true and giving you permission to shoot for Mars where your financial future is concerned.

FINANCIAL FAST TRACK FACT

FAITH COMES BY HEARING (ROMANS 10:17). FAITH FOR ACCELERATED FINANCIAL RESULTS ALSO COMES BY HEARING.

How Philosophies Play with Your Financial Thinking

Plato might be messing with your head. Seriously! He argued that there is a separation between what is physical and what is spiritual. That philosophy is alive and well today. It is called *dualism*. As the Roman empire got its hooks in the church, dualism slowly replaced the Hebraic influence. As a result, spiritual people have been taught to divide their lives into two categories: spiritual and secular or spiritual and material. So, everything you do on Sunday is incredible and awesome.

But when you go to work from Monday through Friday, it's all drudgery in the big, bad, evil world.

Especially in biblical times, the Jewish people saw God's creation in a holistic way that was both physical and spiritual, with no division. When Jews read the Torah and prayed, they were being spiritual. When they did business in the workplace and made money by serving others, they were being spiritual. This might explain why the same Hebrew root, *avad*, describes both a person who is worshiping Yahweh and one who is at work serving clients.[48] Worship, work, and service are covered in the same word. Jews viewed success as a moral and spiritual obligation, and a matter of personal responsibility. We should see it that way too.

The Jewish community in the United States is tiny—just 2.4 percent of the population in 2020.[49] Yet in 2010, when Forbes listed the four hundred richest Americans, thirty of them were Jews. And when "Forbes published its 2018 roster of America's wealthiest," five Jews "made the top 10 list."[50]

Talk about a group that has felt the sting of forces opposing its financial confidence! No people group has been more attacked for their faith than the Jewish people. Yet they stay dedicated to the Torah's concept of spiritual men becoming rich. The idea is deeply embedded in their understanding; therefore, they continue to dominate the "rich lists."

Christians read many of the same Bible stories as their Jewish brothers and sisters, yet Christian billionaires are not as easy to find as Jewish ones. The cross was a great exchange. We trade our sin, sickness, and poverty for God's forgiveness, healing, and riches. But most of us aren't reaping the same financial rewards as our Jewish counterparts.

> *You know the grace of our Lord Jesus Christ, that though He was rich, yet for your sakes He became poor, that you through His poverty might become rich.*
> —2 CORINTHIANS 8:9

It's time to release our religious "emergency brakes" and start living as God intends us to live. That means becoming aware of when we miss the truth. For one thing, we need to learn that poverty isn't a sign of spirituality. The best thing you can do for poor people is not become one. God loves the poor but hates

---

48 *Strong's Hebrew Lexicon*, s.v. "abad," (H5647).

49 "The Size of the U.S. Jewish Population," *Pew Research Center*, 11 May 2021, https://www.pewforum.org/2021/05/11/the-size-of-the-u-s-jewish-population/.

50 "Five Jews Make Forbes' List of Top Ten Wealthiest Americans," *Times of Israel*, 6 Oct. 2018, https://www.timesofisrael.com/5-jews-make-forbes-list-of-top-10-wealthiest-americans/.

poverty. Why? Because it steals your identity, kills your dreams, and destroys your relationships (John 10:10). Extended seasons of poverty will erode your financial confidence by causing you to think negatively about yourself and your future and act on lies that simply are not true.

> *No one would have remembered the Good Samaritan if he'd only had*
> *compassion, good intention, a sermon, prayer, or a scripture to quote. He is*
> *remembered and respected because he had both **mercy** and lots of **money**.*
> —Dr. J

Poverty makes you want to submit, settle, and surrender your dreams. It tries to convince you that you're not enough, you don't deserve to prosper, and *less* is your lot in life. To destroy you psychologically and financially, it chips away your positive self-talk, self-esteem, and self-image. Ultimately, poverty destroys your financial confidence.

That is evil.

Many Christians believe poverty keeps them humble. But staying humble is easy when you're poor. The real test of humility comes when you have wealth and power (Deuteronomy 8:11–17). Plus, poverty often amplifies pride by making you unwilling to hear the truth about your circumstances and possibilities. Say what you want about the wealthy, but they recognize their need of coaching in every area of life.

Have I got your attention? Is it possible you've been hating the wrong villain? Rich and successful people aren't your problem. Money's not your problem. Stop hating on success and money. You repel what you hate. What you attack, you cannot attract. The real villains are poverty and middle-class living. You must develop a hatred, not for the poor but for lack. Then you can smash the chains that keep you from financial abundance.

Poverty is the thief of your dreams. Attack it, and it will flee.

FINANCIAL FAST TRACK FACT

DON'T SHRINK YOUR DREAMS TO THE SIZE OF YOUR CHECKBOOK.

Quit Shrinking Your Thinking

It has been said that "the smaller the head, the bigger the dreams." In other words, children dream big, but as we get older, our dreams shrink. Some of us stop dreaming altogether.

We are born with the capacity to carry a vision and bring it to pass. But as we age, we acclimate to a sense of impossibility. We subdue our desires until we are left with an *almost* life. I believe it's our attempt to cut our dreams down to the size of our paychecks. However, the seed of our potential is often found in our dreams. If we discard our dreams, we kill the seed.

Many of us have done this. We have settled for an *almost* life, an imitation of the real thing. But it's a discounted version of God's intent. It started when somehow, somewhere, we believed a lie. Then, without consciously realizing it, we became experts at living it.

My friend, never protect a belief system that has not produced success, wealth, and happiness in your life. If you fight for your limitations, your limitations will let you win. If you continue fighting against yourself to justify your lies, your lies will have your lunch.

You're in the wrong fight! You should be fighting for your possibilities. You should be fighting for the truth and for reasons to be more successful, wealthier, and happier. That is the battle you were born to wage and win.

Are you ready to fight for your potential? Or will you continue following the masses who have settled for less?

It's your call.

• • • • • • • • • •

FINANCIAL FAST TRACK COACHING

Your *why* gives you the drive to take massive action toward your financial goals. My personal *why* is that I want to make a lot of money, so I can enjoy my life, take good care of my family, and be used by God to serve millions of people. My life's purpose is to help others succeed. Before my body gives out, I want to reach ten million people with this message.

1) What is your financial *why*?

2) Write down *why* you want to be a billionaire or millionaire and how you plan to live that life.

5

PUSH THE ACCELERATOR!
GET CLEAR ON WHAT YOU WANT

y parents divorced when I was eight, so I treasured the weekends when my dad would come get me and spend time with me. I told you about when he showed up in the brand-new Corvette Stingray he bought as a newly single man. That morning, we went to a raceway where he could race other Corvettes. I still remember him in his racing helmet, giving me a thumbs up from the track.

That experience birthed my love of Corvettes and speed. For years, however, I allowed my dream of owning a Corvette to die. It was even bigger than that: I allowed what I call my "want button" to be turned off. I know what that's like, and I hate to see other people living that way.

My job as a coach is to help my clients go from where they are to where they really want to be. That means helping them create a vehicle to get there. But I get paid the big bucks to help them do it fast. If I don't produce, I get fired!

One of my first coaching questions is really four questions rolled together:

What do you want to be?

What do you want to have?

What do you want to do?

Who do you want to help?

I don't just ask questions; I make this bold promise: "If you can tell me what you want, I can help you get it faster than you think possible."

One of the biggest challenges is getting people to decide what they want. For many, the "want button" has been in the "off" position for a long time. Until we get it turned back on, I can't help them. It's a huge step because clarity is powerful. Once they are clear on their wants, their financial confidence kicks in and their minds open up. That's when they figure out how to make their dreams happen.

When I was in my thirties, I lacked clarity. I didn't know what I wanted to be, do, have, and help. I had no targets to aim at. I had no written dreams, goals, or plans. Honestly, I was afraid to think about a big future. I was living a small life and praying the safe, wimpy prayers of the masses like, "Lord, I just want Your will to be done in my life."

That type of prayer is what landed me in financial trouble to begin with.

Different prayers fit different circumstances. The "Your will be done" prayer is a consecration prayer. You're saying, "Lord, I will do what You want me to do, go where You want me to go, and say what You want me to say." That is not the *mountain-moving* faith prayer that brings accelerated results. You don't say this prayer to quickly multiply your income or get that Corvette. It's not that kind of prayer.

Leaving Dreamless Spirituality Behind

Two young men in their twenties came to me for coaching. One was very spiritual, had been raised in a middle-class Christian home, and attended church all his life. The other was raised in an abusive home with very poor parents who never went to church. I asked both men the same question: "What do you want to be, do, have, and help?"

The spiritual man said passively, "I want to get to know God more. I want to do His will. I want to see into the invisible realm and live in God's presence."

The unchurched man answered enthusiastically, in one succinct sentence: "I want to become a millionaire by the time I am thirty!"

Which man do you think I was able to help?

You can have strong values and be dreamless. Many spiritual people get their values mixed up with their dreams and desires. The spiritual man in this case valued prayer, praise, and the Bible, all of which are wonderful. However, I never could get him to mentally break free and decide what he wanted. He was conditioned to believe you cannot be spiritually wealthy and materially wealthy at the same time.

The unchurched man had no such concerns, so he boldly moved forward. He eventually became a spiritual giant and recently bought a $34 million apartment complex. With his wealth, he helps support orphanages around the world. The spiritual guy is still attending church to get more "faith." And he's living in his parents' basement and working for minimum wage.

FINANCIAL FAST TRACK FACT

POOR THEOLOGY CREATES POOR RESULTS AND POORER PEOPLE.

I know this story all too well. I was like that spiritual but clueless young man, and I questioned whether wanting the finer things in life was a right way to live. I wrestled with that ambiguity until I encountered the late Dr. Robert Schuller, who challenged me to become a "possibility thinker."[51] What is that? It is the core belief that you can be more, do more, have more, and help more people.

Remember my mother-in-law's spare bedroom? My life started changing in that little space. That's when I met the challenge of writing my lifelong dreams, desires, and goals on a yellow notepad. On the top of the page, I penned this imagination-stretching question: "What if God said I could do, be, and have whatever I wanted?"

When I was finished writing, my answer was only five pages long. I thought small because I hadn't yet learned to use my imagination. However, within the next ten years, all those wants were fulfilled. What I thought would take my whole life happened in less than a decade. And yes, a new Velocity Yellow, convertible Corvette Stingray was on my *want* list. I still own that car. I don't need it, but I sure enjoy it. I keep it as a constant reminder that God supplies my needs and cares about my wants.

*Delight yourself also in the LORD, and He shall give you the **desires** of your heart.*
—PSALMS 37:4

---

51 Robert H. Schuller, *It's Possible* (Grand Rapids, MI: F. H. Revell, 1978).

The abundant life is not dreamless; it's full and vibrant. God will give you the desires of your heart when you delight in Him. If you want a theological understanding of the subject, read the Gospels. You will discover that Jesus never asked people what they needed. He asked, "What do you *want* Me to do?"—not because He didn't know the answer but because He was the ultimate coach. He knew they had to decide what they wanted. And once they did, it manifested *fast*.

What if Jesus showed up at your house today and asked, "What do you want Me to do for you?" Would you know exactly what to ask of Him? Remember that He's asking *what you want*.

Think about Jesus' first recorded miracle. It happened when He was at a wedding, and the guests finished all the wine at the open bar (John 2). Did they need more wine? No! In fact, Scripture warns against drinking too much of it. But the wedding guests *wanted* more. Obviously, there is more to this miracle than the people's wants, but the fact is that Jesus performed a *want* miracle—and it came *fast*.

If God already has your needs in mind (which He does), your next higher question should be, "Exactly what do I want? Have I asked for it yet? Am I taking action to see it come to pass?"

I believe that knowing what we want and asking for it are more important than we realize. I have been in every kind of church you can imagine, from a tiny house church in the countryside to big-city megachurches with 50,000 or more in attendance. Often, I scan the audience and ask myself, *Why are there so many depressed-looking Christians, yet so many happy sinners?* Does that question bother you? It bothers me because Christians shouldn't be more depressed than sinners. Proverbs 13:12 says, "Hope deferred makes the heart sick, *but when the desire comes, it is a tree of life.*" With so many Christians looking glum, I can only conclude that their desires aren't coming, so they are sick.

But why? Don't most Christians know that God wants to meet their needs?

Yes. They do. Yet they are afraid to ask for more than their needs. Unless you are living in utter deprivation, getting your needs met doesn't unlock your joy. When my wife comes home from grocery shopping and hands me deodorant, toothpaste, and toilet paper, I'm thankful that my needs have been met. But those things don't make me jump and shout.

I suspect that's where most Christians live. They've got their deodorant, toothpaste, and toilet paper, but they haven't thought about, asked for, or received what they really want. They are plodding along in a spiritual but dreamless wilderness.

Most nonspiritual people aren't hindered by religious belief systems. They're missing out on the greatest need of all, which is a relationship with God, but they don't know it. They just go after what they want and feel happy when they get it.

We never test the resources of God until we attempt the impossible.[52]
—F. B. MEYER

I'm not saying that Christians are incapable of dreaming. Dolly Parton was raised in a Pentecostal family and has an incredible story. One of twelve children, she grew up in a small log cabin in the Appalachian Mountains.[53] There she became a full-fledged possibility thinker. Her dreams have manifested in spades: She has written some five thousand songs since childhood.[54] She's a country music icon, accomplished actress, and best-selling author. She wrote massive hits, including "Jolene" and Whitney Houston's chartbuster, "I Will Always Love You." In her song, "Somebody's Everything,"[55] Parton asks whether expecting everything is expecting too much. She has proved that it's not. Her possibility thinking has paid off!

The Law of Acceleration

Deciding what you want and taking massive action activates the Law of Acceleration in your life. Dolly Parton didn't achieve massive success by accident. She owned her wants, and acceleration happened. Did you know that she wrote "Jolene" and "I Will Always Love You" in the same day?[56] Can you imagine the financial windfall that was? It was the Law of Acceleration at work!

When you decide what you want and start moving toward it, your desired outcome rapidly moves toward you! The more action you take and the faster you move in the direction of your dreams, goals, and desires, the faster they move in your direction.

Draw near to God and He will draw near to you.
—JAMES 4:8

---

52   "Forty-Six F. B. Meyer Quotes," *Christian Quotes*, accessed September 22, 2021, https://www.christianquotes.info/quotes-by-author/f-b-meyer-quotes/.

53   Graham Hoppe, "Icon and Identity: Dolly Parton's Hillbilly Appeal," *Southern Cultures*, accessed September 22, 2021, https://www.southerncultures.org/article/icon-identity-dolly-partons-hillbilly-appeal/.

54   Killian Fox, "Me and the Muse: Dolly Parton on Her Inspirations," *Guardian*, 4 Sep. 2016, https://www.theguardian.com/music/2016/sep/04/dolly-parton-me-muse-inspirations-pure-and-simple.

55   Dolly Parton, "Somebody's Everything," Sony/ATV Music Publishing.

56   Mathew Rodriquez, "Dolly Parton Wrote 'Jolene' and 'I Will Always Love You' in One Day," *Out*, 19 March 2019, https://www.out.com/music/2019/3/19/dolly-parton-wrote-jolene-and-i-will-always-love-you-one-day.

The starting point for achieving your financial target is *desire*. Being successful requires a burning desire for what you want. Without it, you cannot produce the energy and internal drive you need to overcome the external forces that will challenge your climb up the financial mountain (more on this in coming chapters).

That means you must state your desires. A Harvard study conducted between 1979 and 1989 concluded that only 3 percent of Harvard MBA graduates had clear goals about what they wanted to achieve.[57] That tells me that the other 97 percent were unsure of their desires or unwilling to own them. As researchers followed this class for ten years, they found that the 3 percent had incomes ten times greater than the other 97 percent combined.

Push the Accelerator

When I first got my five hundred-horsepower Stingray Corvette, I was reluctant to punch it. Guys with Mustangs often tried to race me at red lights, and I always let them take off without me. One day, I took one of my Corvette buddies out for a ride. He had a lower horsepower engine and wanted to see how fast my car was compared with his.

I drove down the road like I was driving my Mercedes. My friend looked at me and shouted, "Come on, man! Punch it! Push the accelerator to the floor. Let's see how fast this thing can go!"

I found out that the car could blow my head back and go from zero to sixty in less than three seconds—*if* I hit the accelerator.

||||||||||||||||||||||||| **FINANCIAL FAST TRACK FACT** |||||||||||||||||||||||||

YOU WON'T GET ANYWHERE BY FLOORING THE ACCELERATOR AND BRAKE AT THE SAME TIME.

Hesitation kept me from experiencing the power of the car I had long dreamed of owning. What's keeping you from deciding what you want? Why aren't you pressing the accelerator on your financial future?

---

57 Annabel Acton, "How to Set Goals (And Why You Should Write Them Down)," *Forbes*, 3 Nov. 2017, https://www.forbes.com/sites/annabelacton/2017/11/03/how-to-set-goals-and-why-you-should-do-it/?sh=7224be98162d.

Don't be too embarrassed to answer. Whatever is keeping you in "slow mode" is keeping other people there too. I have run into six common but flawed belief systems that keep people from punching the gas. They might be keeping you from racing to your results, so let's check them out.

Wrong Belief #1: "To Want Is Wrong"

If you believe it's wrong to want, you have company. Unfortunately, you are going to need permission to progress. When you don't decide what you want, you become a victim of circumstances instead of the beneficiary of divine possibilities.

Let me walk you through a coaching process on this subject. Just answer my questions and see what happens.

» Is it wrong for a homeless person to want to move into a trailer park?

» Is it wrong for someone in India who walks to work every day to want a bicycle, motorcycle, or used car?

» Is it wrong for a person who rents a one-bedroom apartment in a rough part of the inner city to want a two-bedroom house in the suburbs?

» Is it wrong for a middle-class person to want to move into a gated community for added protection?

» Is it wrong for a person who lives in a gated community to want to move into a mansion?

» Is it wrong for a person who lives at poverty level to want to make $40,000 a year?

» Is it wrong for a person who makes $40,000 to want $100,000?

» Is it wrong for a person who makes $100,000 to want to make $1 million or $1 billion?

The answer to all these questions is *no*! It's not wrong to want a better lifestyle. You are not crazy for wanting more. In fact, the crazy people are the ones who claim not to want something better in life. They justify their "selfish" and "comfortable" lifestyle because they don't want more for themselves or others.

Psalms 23:1 says, "The LORD is my shepherd; I shall not want." I used to interpret that in a negative way, as I "should not want." I used it to justify what I already believed. But that is not the meaning at all! If God is my Shepherd, and I am acting on His principles, all my needs and wants will be met, and I won't want for anything.

The Hebrew words translated "not want" are *loh* and *echsar*, which together mean, "not" "have a need" or "diminish."[58] To the Jews, *want* goes beyond the place of need. So, who should be in want? Proverbs 13:25 says, "The righteous eats to the satisfying of his soul, but the stomach of the *wicked* shall be in *want*."

Does that settle the issue for you? It should.

Wrong Belief #2: "I Know What I Don't Want"

When I ask coaching clients, "What do you want to be, do, have, and help?" I cannot tell you how many of them respond with a laundry list of things they don't want. They say, "Dr. J, I don't want to get divorced; I don't want to be poor; I don't want to be unhappy, sick, alone, overweight, or single, and I don't want to work at this same job forever."

If you list the things you don't want, guess what? You will attract more of those things. Where your focus goes, your energy flows, and your results show. That's why you keep getting more of what you are trying to lose.

It's time for that kind of insanity to stop.

When I was pressing to expand my business, I consulted with my friend Les Brown. He encouraged me, saying, "Life is a fight for territory. You must fight for what you want, or what you don't want will take over and win."

True hope is having a confident expectation that your future will be better than your present. Worry is having a negative picture of what you don't want to happen and running it through your mind again and again. And what happens? Everything you worried about comes to pass.

Wrong Belief #3: "I Don't Want Anything"

After I spoke about this subject one day, a little old lady scolded me. "Young man," she said, "I don't want anything. I am happy and content. I have a roof over my head. I have clothes to wear and shoes on my feet. I have plenty to eat and a home in heaven when I die."

At first, I thought, *Maybe I am greedy for wanting more.* Then I heard a voice within me say, *She is the selfish and greedy one.* I thought, *How's that?* The voice answered, *She has food to eat, but is unconcerned with those who are hungry. She has shoes on her feet, but what about the barefoot?* That woman's potential overflow could have blessed others. But that's a lesson for another day. Most people who say they don't want anything are only justifying—to themselves and others—their small thinking

---

58 Blue Letter Bible, accessed September 22, 2021, https://www.blueletterbible.org/lexicon/h3808/kjv/wlc/0-1/ and https://www.blueletterbible.org/lexicon/h2637/kjv/wlc/0-1/.

and lack. They have settled for a lifestyle that requires no mountain-moving faith to accomplish. Then they pretend to be proud of their underachievement.

> *There is no reward in this world for settling for something you don't want!*[59]
> —JOHN COUGAR MELLENCAMP

Wrong Belief #4: "I Know What I Want, But. . . ."

Unlike the previous group, this crowd knows exactly what they want. However, they maintain what I call a "but list":

*"I would like to drive a brand-new car paid for in cash, **but**. . . ."*
*"I'd love to quit this job and open a BBQ food truck, **but**. . . ."*
*"I thought about owning a home, **but**. . . ."*

The "but" people remind me of the man at the Pool of Bethesda who waited by the water thirty-eight years to be the first person in when the healing angel touched the pool (John 5). When Jesus asked him what he wanted, he explained his "but": "I want to be healed, but I have no one to put me in the water."

Losers create excuses. Winners create bridges of possibility.

Everything after your "but" is an excuse you have been playing inside your head, possibly for a lifetime. Until you identify and eliminate it, you will not experience life at the level God has in mind.

Many excuses are money excuses:

*I want to start a business, **but** I don't have the money.*
*I want to be a speaker, coach, and author, **but** I can't afford the training.*
*I want to go on a decent vacation, **but** my budget won't let me.*

The issue is never about a lack of resources. It's always about whether you are resourceful. It goes back to financial confidence. The resourceful, financially confident mind says, "I know what I want, and I will find the money to make it happen."

Your "but" prevents you from taking 100 percent responsibility for your financial situation, and it puts the blame on someone or something else. This renders you powerless over your own life. You cannot control every circumstance, but when you take responsibility for your finances, you can reclaim control.

You will either be obsessed with what you want or become obsessed with excuses for why you didn't get it. You can play that pitiful game for a lifetime. As my personal trainer always says, "Excuses are the nails that build the house of failure."

Make the decision that success is your sole responsibility.

---

59   David Masciotra, "No Depression: John Mellencamp; Plain Spoken—A Documentary of the Human Spirit," *John Mellencamp News*, 15 Feb. 2018, https://www.mellencamp.com/news.html?n_id=2962.

Wrong Belief #5: "Wanting Hurts Too Much"

Have you ever wanted something very badly? You asked for it, you prayed for it, and you worked your butt off for it—but you didn't get it. Did it hurt? Of course! Disappointment is painful, and we naturally want to move away from pain. The problem is that we attribute the pain to the desire instead of the disappointing outcome. Therefore, we buy into a belief system that says, "It's easier not to want anything at all."

This is another entry point into learned hopelessness. Remember that hope deferred makes the heart sick. I believe this sickness has become an invisible ceiling to the middle class. Ambition does have a price: it results in both successes and failures. Wanting comes with risks, but you have a 50 percent chance of achieving a positive outcome. Unless you accept the risk of wanting, your chances of failure are 100 percent.

Wanting is not painful; it is energizing. Loss and disappointment are painful, but they are part of a fulfilling life. The price of no ambition is 100 percent disappointment and unfulfilled potential. Keep the following equations in mind:

» **Disappointment = pain**
» **Wanting = some risk**
» **Not wanting anything = total risk of failure**

Wrong Belief #6: "I Want More!"

When I ask people what they want, they often answer in generic terms, saying, "I want more money."

So, I reach into my pocket, hand them a nickel, and say, "Your prayer has been answered."

When they give me the side-eye, I ask, "Why aren't you jumping for joy? You got what you wanted, didn't you?"

That's when it dawns on them—they need to be more specific. Just praying for "more" or for "increase" is too easy and vague.

When Hannah was barren for years, she had the confidence to ask God for exactly what she wanted, "I want a son," she said.

She could have said, "At this point, I'll take any baby You've got." However, she made up her mind and was very specific. She described a certain child and promised that she would give him to the Lord's service (1 Samuel 1:9–11). What she did not realize was that God wanted a new priesthood. Hannah's desire and God's desire matched!

Is it possible that you have been financially barren because God is bringing you to a place of confidently identifying what you want, asking Him for it, and working to make it happen?

> *Most people are not going after what they want. Even some of the most serious goal seekers and goal setters, they're going after what they think they can get.*[60]
> —BOB PROCTOR

To push the accelerator, you must be clear about your wants. Most people don't live the lives they want. They live what they stumble into. You are called to abundance. But you *must* decide. It is time to ask God, ask yourself, and ask of life that which you truly want, not what you think you can get.

Turn on your *want* button!

---

60   "Bob Proctor Quotes, AZ Quotes, accessed September 22, 2021, https://www.azquotes.com/author/37901-Bob_Proctor.

• • • • • • • • • •

FINANCIAL FAST TRACK COACHING

To get clear on what you want, take these imagineAction steps:

1) First, set your new target.

   Ask yourself: "What kind of lifestyle do I want in my future?"

   Describe that lifestyle, in detail, in writing.

2) Second, reverse engineer the future life you imagine by asking yourself:

   What must I do to live as I just described?

   How can I make a million dollars in a year? (Put it in writing!)

   What knowledge do I need?

   What skills do I need?

   What mindset do I need?

   What habits do I need to form?

   What relationships do I need to cultivate?

   Which mentors do I need to engage?

3) Third, create what you see in your imagination.

Commit to three things you will do in the next ninety days to bring 50 percent of your one-year financial goals to pass.

1. _____

2. _____

3. _____

4) Fourth, don't tuck away your notes. Keep them front of mind. Stay out of the theoretical and get into action!

FINANCIAL
FAST TRACK

| 1 | 2 | 3 | 4 | 5 | 6 | 7 |

Live in the Future Today | Elevate Your Value

6

ELEVATE YOUR VALUE:
BE MORE GENEROUS,
SERVE MORE OF GOD'S CHILDREN

B onnie and I love Disney World, the happiest place on earth. I confess that standing in long lines on a certain blistering day in Florida wasn't quite my happy place. In fact, it felt a little like hell!

The first ride we chose had two lines. The very short line was called FastPass (it's now called Disney Genie). People on that line scanned their tickets and queued up for quick access. Then there was my line—the general admission line where we waited ninety minutes to have sixty seconds of fun. With all that waiting, we missed many rides and attractions. However, I experienced abundantly sore feet and a stiff back.

I thought, *I hate it here. What's happy about this?* When we exited the park, I stopped at the information desk and asked about the price of a FastPass. The young lady replied, "It's free, sir. Just check in and schedule the attractions you wish to ride."

Relief and anger washed over me all at once. I thought, *Are you kidding me?* So, the next day, we went to Epcot and checked in for FastPass. Our experience was very different from the previous day. We stood in those nice short lines and hopped on each ride almost immediately. At the end of that day, I said, "I'm happy and can't wait to come back!"

The following morning, I sat on the hotel balcony overlooking the park. As I sipped my coffee, I asked myself these Financial Fast Track Questions: *How many times have I missed out because I lacked the information to make the right decisions? How often have I been stuck in the slow lane when I could have accessed the Fast Track to success?* Does that question ring your bell? It did mine.

What God Isn't Doing

You know what traffic jams are like. You change lanes because that other lane looks faster than yours. Then the new lane comes to a standstill, and frustration builds. It's the same at the supermarket. You run in to buy a last-minute item for your cookout. Then you hurry to the shortest checkout line. When the cashier calls for a price check, the shortest line becomes the slowest, and you feel "chosen" for a delay.

In everyday situations, we make decisions the best way we know how, and some of them backfire. When I was at my lowest point financially, I thought God was deciding who would be successful and who wouldn't. Because all the supposedly "right things" I was doing had not worked, I assumed that God had picked me for the slow line. In my mind, that had to be the problem.

FINANCIAL FAST TRACK FACT

IT IS YOUR DECISIONS—NOT YOUR CONDITIONS—THAT SHAPE THE FUTURE OUTCOME OF YOUR LIFE.

I was conditioned to think that if I lived righteously, went to church, read my Bible every day, prayed, listened to worship music, and tithed to my church, I would attract God's favor. Someday, He would wave His mighty hand and doors of opportunity would fly open for me. Financial breakthroughs would show up, and fat checks would appear in my mailbox.

That didn't happen, but it wasn't God's fault. He wasn't determining my level of success or financial prosperity—I was! If that still sounds like blasphemy to you, consider the fact that if God controlled everyone's financial outcomes:

» Missionaries would be billionaires. Intercessors would be praying in mansions. Foster children would live in gated communities with caring parents. Widows and widowers would be well cared for. Senior citizens would not die in dingy nursing homes. Every church would be debt free. Pastoring would be the highest-paid profession on the planet.

And if God were really deciding how much money each person will have:

» Drug dealers would be bankrupt. Casinos would be shut down. Lottery tickets wouldn't exist. Pimps would have no prostitutes to exploit. Pornography websites would fold. Corrupt governments and politicians would be out of business.

Clearly, God does not decide who gets what money. He doesn't give you wealth; He "gives you *power to get wealth*" (Deuteronomy 8:18). Your financial future is shaped by your daily decisions to exercise His principles. Hidden within them are the results you long to experience. God does not assign some people to wealth and others to poverty. He simply honors His principles for those who do the same.

FINANCIAL FAST TRACK FACT

YOU CAN DO WHAT IS RIGHT BY GIVING 10 PERCENT OF YOUR INCOME, BUT IF YOU MAKE BAD DECISIONS WITH THE OTHER 90 PERCENT, YOU WILL STAY BROKE.

Confidence and Value

This leads us to a key piece of information and a decision every one of us must make before we can reach a new financial level; it is the decision to elevate our value.

The cold, hard truth is that the marketplace doesn't pay you what you want. It pays what you deserve, based on your value. In my mother-in-law's house, I had the potential to be worth millions of dollars, which was exactly what I wanted. Yet, the marketplace set my value at $30,000. When I decided to elevate my value, the marketplace recognized that I deserved six figures, and within two years, it delivered what I deserved.

Ten years later, I sat staring at my phone for almost fifteen minutes, pondering my next call. It was to a business owner who had stagnated at $500,000 in annual profits but wanted to break the million-dollar mark. I had framed a coaching proposal and was about to present it to him. I planned to ask $120,000 for one year of coaching.

I must admit, I experienced an internal confidence war. I kept thinking, *This is how much my first house cost. Who would pay that much for a few hours' interaction each month?* My ask seemed almost ridiculous. So, I considered lowering the number. *Maybe I should charge him $50,000. That's still a good chunk for coaching.* Then I recognized the voice of my own self-worth and knew what I needed to do. I picked up the phone and confidently made my $120,000 proposal. Then I shut my mouth and listened for the client's response.

Immediately, he shot back, "Well, you are America's #1 Confidence Coach. If you can't help me, I'm in big trouble. Can we schedule our first session for next week?"

Of course, I said what any smart professional would say: "Well, let me check my schedule."

Confidence matters! I received what I was worth, and he received a nice return on investment. During that year of coaching, my client exceeded his desired goal and jumped from $500,000 in annual profits to $1.3 million.

FINANCIAL FAST TRACK FACT

WE GET PAID FOR BRINGING VALUE TO THE MARKETPLACE.

How the Marketplace Works

The marketplace doesn't function on fairness. If it did, top talents would always make the most money. The world is full of highly talented people who are undiscovered or grossly underpaid. The marketplace neither cares about that, nor does it function on spirituality. If it did, intercessors really would be praying in mansions.

Listen, it takes time to bring value to the marketplace, but we don't get paid for time. If you say, "I am making $25 per hour," that's not quite true. If it were, you could stay home watching cartoons, and whoever is paying you would still send the money.

Has that been your experience? No. You don't get paid for your time; you get paid for the value you put into that time. Instead of asking how you can raise your hourly earnings, you need to learn how to raise your value.

FINANCIAL FAST TRACK QUESTION

IS IT POSSIBLE TO DOUBLE, TRIPLE, OR EVEN 10X THE VALUE AND SKILLS YOU BRING TO THE MARKETPLACE?

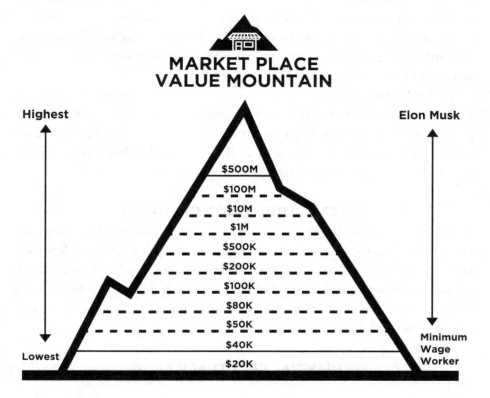

MARKET PLACE
VALUE MOUNTAIN

American economics are simple and unique. You are on a financial mountain, and you have to climb it. Most of us start at the bottom, earning minimum wage in our teens. But that's only the starting point. You don't pitch a tent and build a life there. Your assignment is to keep climbing until you reach the top of the mountain.

Hall of Fame quarterback Roger Staubach says, "There are no traffic jams along the extra mile."[61]

He's right. You won't find many people climbing to the financial mountaintop. Most of them settle for making it halfway. So, how do you leave the pack behind and keep climbing? The goal is to progressively increase your value and consistently offer that value to the marketplace. The "normal" climb is incremental. Step by step, you gain knowledge, recognize your difference, get more experience, serve more people, solve more problems, become an expert, and multiply your skills. However, the right coach can help you move from small steps to quantum leaps. Instead of inching your value and income upward, you can blast through levels.

Consider Elon Musk. As CEO, he earned $595 million in 2019 (and way more in 2020). Can you imagine receiving the equivalent of $11,442,308 per week? Why would a company pay a CEO that kind of money? Is anyone worth that much?

The answer is, "Yes!" If your company's CEO can get bring in billions in government grants, you will gladly pay him what Musk is making. That's a small investment for a very large return.

The harder question to ask is why a company would pay someone $8 per hour. It comes down to value: the $8 per hour person isn't very valuable to the marketplace, at least not yet. You might be a valuable member of the church. You are definitely invaluable in the sight of God. But if the marketplace says you're only worth $8 per hour, it won't pay you high-earner money.

Elevate Your Value of Money

Money doesn't symbolize power. If it did, all poor people would be powerless to change and would be doomed to live forever as hopeless victims. Money is a byproduct of value creation and represents an exchange of value between people or entities. Money isn't value in and of itself; money represents value based on the perceptions of those who exchange it. Money is simply a means of exchange and a representation of value that has been added.

‖‖‖‖‖‖‖‖‖‖‖‖‖‖‖‖‖‖‖‖‖ **FINANCIAL FAST TRACK FACT** ‖‖‖‖‖‖‖‖‖‖‖‖‖‖‖‖‖‖‖‖‖

MONEY IS A SYMBOL OF THE VALUE YOU CREATE FOR OTHERS.

---

61 Shep Hyken, "There's No Traffic Jam on the Extra Mile," *Forbes*, 27 Feb. 2016, https://www.forbes.com/sites/shephyken/2016/02/27/theres-no-traffic-jam-on-the-extra-mile/?sh=418dc9b979a6.

If you are convinced that rapidly elevating your finances is wrong, you will never properly assess your value or increase it. Therefore, you will not unleash your full potential to serve others. That's a problem because your prosperity comes from applying your value and fulfilling your destiny. Serving others is integral to your destiny.

Making hyperspiritual claims is a problem too. People say things like, "Take the world, but give me Jesus. I don't need money." What they are really saying is, "I have no intention of providing value to anyone but myself." There is certainly no prosperity in that.

In kingdom economics, no one is an island unto themselves, as the following three pillars of kingdom economics show:

Pillar #1 is stewardship or managing the resources of another person.

Pillar #2 is investment or taking what God has given you and multiplying it.

Pillar #3 is generosity, or giving, which is the only proof that you have conquered greed and selfishness.

We will talk about investing later, and the case for generosity speaks for itself. But without stewardship, there are no second and third pillars. It isn't rocket science. Good stewards keep good accounts and know what the numbers are. They value money enough to keep their eyes on it—not the way Ebenezer Scrooge did, but in a way that honors provision.

I'm amazed by people who go to church every Sunday but have no idea what their bank balances are until they check them. I'm equally amazed by those who never check but keep writing rubber checks for their tithes and offerings.

Believe it or not, I understand how it happens. It's a matter of mixing faith and facts with fiction and fantasy. When Bonnie and I were $180,000 in debt, we gave to our church and spoke positive confessions over our finances. We thought we were living by faith, but we were living in denial. That seemed easier because every time we discussed our money problems, World War III broke out.

Instead of fighting, we swept our money problems under the rug and lived a fictional life on our private fantasy island. Because we loved and valued God, we thought we had to devalue money. We said money wasn't important, and we used God to justify our lousy stewardship.

That wasn't faith. Faith doesn't deny the facts. You cannot move mountains by denying their existence. Real faith faces the facts and then activates a plan to change them.

So, we decided to hire an accountant. Everything we'd spent years covering up came into the light. Shame and guilt had long prevented us from owning our financial condition. Our accountant took away some of the sting after he saw our books and said, "Ah, this isn't so bad. I have seen people a lot worse off than you."

Once we started valuing money, we embraced our responsibility as stewards by keeping our eyes on what money we had. That's when the floodgates opened. Because we were faithful with a small amount, God could trust us to steward more.

‖‖‖‖‖‖‖‖‖‖‖‖‖‖‖‖‖‖‖‖ **FINANCIAL FAST TRACK FACT** ‖‖‖‖‖‖‖‖‖‖‖‖‖‖‖‖‖‖‖‖

FACE THE FACTS, AND GET ON THE FINANCIAL FAST TRACK!

No Fear

Are you getting the importance of value? "Have you faced the facts about your money? Do you know your numbers?" If not, go ahead and look. The numbers are what they are. Knowing them might sting, but it will also help you.

People have lots of fears about money, but you don't need to be afraid. Remember that money isn't evil. Money is paper that symbolizes value. It's up to you not to use evil methods to acquire it. Like Dr. Mike Murdock said years ago, "If money was evil, the devil would dump an entire Brinks truckload of money on your front lawn today. If money is evil, why did God double Job's money at the end of his life?"[62]

Money is energy waiting to be used, and the person who uses it determines whether it's good or not. Part of our confusion about money's "nature" comes from two wicked strategies the enemy has used to keep God's people afraid:

Strategy # 1 is to get good people with tremendous earning potential to believe that their desire for money is evil.

Strategy # 2 is to convince evil people that their desire for money is really good.

These strategies are producing two common conditions: (1) good people lacking the money to do great things and (2) ungodly people controlling money and using it wickedly. It's really that simple. If you use money in evil ways, you might get rich, but you'll reap the whirlwind. If you shun money based on the enemy's lies, you'll compromise your God-given assignment and your well-being.

---

62 Mike Murdoch, "School of Wisdom" seminar, Tampa, Florida, 2003.

||||||||||||||||||||||||||||| **FINANCIAL FAST TRACK FACT** |||||||||||||||||||||||||||||

MONEY IS GOOD BECAUSE IT INCREASES
YOUR REACH, INFLUENCE, AND IMPACT.

Greed, Ambition, and Service

Many people are afraid of money because they fear being called "greedy" or "ambitious." Those words do not mean the same thing. Understanding the difference will liberate your mindset.

Are you ready?

Greed is evil and always seeks something for nothing. The greedy desire more than their share and want it to come at someone else's expense. That is wicked. In the right hands, ambition is good and only seeks gain by serving others. Healthy ambition expects to earn righteously by adding value, solving problems, and helping others to improve their lot.

If you were to stand before a large crowd and say, "Rich people are greedy and love money," most people would agree with you. However, if you dared to say, "People on welfare and those who perpetually seek government handouts are greedy and love money," you might get booed off the stage.

I'm not saying that rich folks never get greedy. I'm simply saying that greed exists in all economic classes. Those who can serve themselves and others by working but choose government assistance instead are as greedy as those who game the marketplace. Even the pressure of living from paycheck to paycheck can foster greed by causing us to forget that life is about giving. That kind of hamster-wheel existence drives us to be self-consumed and self-centered.

Do you remember when Jesus' disciples argued in Luke 22 about who would be considered great in the kingdom? Jesus didn't rebuke them for having ambition; He said those who serve are the greatest in the kingdom. Jesus did more than talk about serving, however. He gave His life for the masses, not just His family and inner circle.

To be great, find a way to serve and add value for as many people as you possibly can. As Zig Ziglar said, "You can have everything you want in life if you help enough other people get what they want."[63]

---

63 "True Joy," Ziglar, accessed September 23, 2021, https://www.ziglar.com/quotes/true-joy/.

⊣⊢⊢⊢⊢⊢⊢⊢⊢⊢⊢⊢⊢⊢⊢⊢⊢ **FINANCIAL FAST TRACK FACT** ⊢⊢⊢⊢⊢⊢⊢⊢⊢⊢⊢⊢⊢⊢⊢⊢⊢

SERVICE TO THE MASSES LEADS TO GREATNESS AND FINANCIAL REWARDS.

Know What Spirituality Is For

People always ask me, "How have you achieved so much success in life?" The answer isn't complicated. Since my financial crash, a changed mindset has empowered me to have influence in the church and the marketplace.

First, however, I had to unlearn some things. I had to realize that successful, powerful, and wealthy people are not inherently worldly or wicked. I had to reevaluate what I'd heard from the pulpit—that true success is about becoming more spiritual. Yes, we are spiritual beings, but you cannot influence the marketplace purely by being spiritual. We no longer live in a culture that highly values and celebrates spirituality. That is unfortunate, but it is reality.

⊣⊢⊢⊢⊢⊢⊢⊢⊢⊢⊢⊢⊢⊢⊢⊢⊢ **FINANCIAL FAST TRACK FACT** ⊢⊢⊢⊢⊢⊢⊢⊢⊢⊢⊢⊢⊢⊢⊢⊢⊢

IN THE CHURCH, YOU GAIN INFLUENCE BY BEING SPIRITUAL. IN THE MARKETPLACE, YOU GAIN INFLUENCE BY BEING SUCCESSFUL.

If you ask your boss for a raise, does your boss say, "Sing 'Amazing Grace,' preach me a sermon, and I will give you a raise"?

No. Your boss says, "Bring more value, experience, knowledge, and skills to the table and I will pay you more." In other words, be of more service to this organization, and you will become more valuable.

Please hear me. I am not knocking the church, pastors, or theologians. Their assignment is to increase people's knowledge of God. They are experts at growing your spirituality, and that will serve you well. But you are reading this book because you need help growing financially. That is my area of expertise and my way of serving others.

|||||||||||||||||||||||||||||| **FINANCIAL FAST TRACK FACT** ||||||||||||||||||||||||||||||

IT'S YOUR MORAL AND SPIRITUAL OBLIGATION TO BECOME A SUCCESS.

Defining Success

Success is defined many ways, mostly involving the achievement of one's desired aims or objectives. Allow me then to define *success* from my perspective. In Dr. Johnson's dictionary, *success* means:

1) Knowing my God-given assignment.
2) Maximizing my potential.
3) Making progress toward achieving my future goals by hitting my daily targets.
4) The feeling I get from achieving my big goals.
5) Sowing seeds that benefit others.

For me, success starts with understanding and fulfilling my God-given assignment. I can have goals, but if I achieve things God didn't call me to do, I am a failure. Because my assignment is bigger than me, maximizing my potential means that I must continually grow. Much of that growth comes from confidently setting *big* goals. I grow, internally and externally, because those goals require massive action. When that action produces the desired results, I feel good and must do what God does—benefit as many people as I can by giving and adding value.

Remember that we are not dualists. Therefore, our success is not limited to one realm. I have learned that being successful means impacting the church and the marketplace. We do this by being spiritual and successful. Like everything else I have learned, and everything we have discussed so far, this kind of success comes down to choices.

It is time to harness the power of your decisions. They will, after all, decide the speed of your cash flow, the fulfillment of your destiny, and the health of your relationships, not to mention the state of your health, wealth, and happiness.

Elevating your value is a decision. Next, let's see what that means.

. . . .

FINANCIAL FAST TRACK COACHING

1) You cannot elevate your personal value without first assessing your current value.

   What is the financial value the marketplace has set for you at this time?

2) Is increasing your value a priority? Are you willing to work to increase it?

3) Consider the following three values and how you view them:

   » Yourself/your self-worth

   Have you decided that you are worthy of success and an abundant life? What convinced you?

   Have you been taught that you are undeserving of happiness, wealth, and success? Who told you those things, and what are their qualifications for saying them?

   Have you been discounting your personal value? Are you going to stop discounting yourself? How?

   » Valuing money

   Money answers everything. If it's a "thing," money can answer it. Have you come to terms with the fact that money is valuable to you?

How will you become a better steward and start keeping an eye on your money?

Have you decided to raise your value of money? How?

» Valuing success

Achievement magnifies your influence and impact. What are your three biggest successes?

Do you celebrate your success? How?

Do you celebrate the success of others? How?

How does/how will success provide and/or increase your influence in the marketplace?

7

FIVE DECISIONS TO ELEVATE YOUR VALUE: LEAVING THE CULT OF MEDIOCRITY

I remember it like it was yesterday. I had just finished unloading the U-Haul and piling our remaining possessions in my mother-in-law's tiny kitchen. There wasn't much left, just some boxes of clothes, a card table, and a chair.

One thought haunted me: *I have nothing. I am nothing. My life is over.* And I was only thirty-five.

Yet, somehow, a powerful truth penetrated my misery: *We don't have to wait until we are rich to prosper.* When all the external, material stuff was stripped away, the only thing Bonnie and I had left was our human value. But it was all we needed. With it, we could create increase by adding value for others. That's how the marketplace works. Much of our human value rested in things we could not see. We had to learn to see them.

Fast-forward to a coaching session with a brokenhearted client of mine. She sobbed as she recounted her divorce. "He took everything! He got the house, the furniture, all the money, and the business. I have nothing. I am trapped in a one-bedroom apartment, eating off paper plates and sleeping on an inflatable mattress. That's it. That's all I have."

I asked her, "Did he steal your imagination? Did he walk away with your ability to dream? Your gifts and talents? Your human worth?"

"Well, no."

"Then he didn't take everything, did he? With what you have left, you can get back what you lost, *sevenfold*."

I am not a product of my circumstances in life. I am a product of my decisions.[64]
—STEPHEN COVEY

Five Decisions

You can create value in the now, whatever *now* looks like. The more value you add, the more prosperous you will be. Wealth is a byproduct of value creation, and it hinges on five decisions. This is not theory; it is advice from a guy who's not worrying about the bills. These decisions increased my value and accelerated my success when all seemed lost. That is the power of what I am about to share.

Decision #1: Elevate Your Standards

When I lost "everything," one thing remained: it was the power of my volition, my God-given permission and ability to decide. The most important decision I made was to elevate my standards. I knew nothing could change until I expected better *from* myself and *for* myself. I had to decide what I would and would not tolerate in my financial life.

FINANCIAL FAST TRACK FACT

YOU CANNOT CHANGE WHAT YOU ARE WILLING TO TOLERATE.

If you tolerate making $30,000 a year, you will never make $60,000. If you tolerate earnings of $120,000, you won't clear $1 million. What you tolerate will dominate. You must get disgusted with your current salary and decide that it won't

---

64   Stephen R. Covey (@StephenRCovey), Twitter, February 24, 2018, 10:01 a.m., https://twitter.com/stephenrcovey/status/967414111666569226?lang=en.

do. Remember: disgust is a powerful emotion and a sharp tool in elevating your standards. So, go ahead—get good and disgusted with the status quo.

Unless you want a dog's life, you cannot afford to settle. If I asked, "Do dogs like bones?"

Most people would say, "Of course they do."

The truth is that dogs love meat, but they settle for the bones.

Many people feel stuck with the "bones" because they got accustomed to doing without "meat." After a while, bones are all they think about. It never crosses their mind that they don't have to settle. It's like the adage says: "Human beings are like dust; they tend to settle."

Stop tolerating. Elevate your financial expectations.

Decision #2: Elevate Your Strength

When I travel, people ask, "How did you start your confidence coaching brand? How did you come up with the idea?"

It's a great question. The brand started in 2002. My wife and I and my personal coach were sitting in my mother-in-law's living room strategizing next steps for my speaking business. Out of the blue, I asked them a simple question, and it produced a multimillion-dollar answer.

"What is my number one greatest strength?"

My coach fired away. "Here's what I know about you: whenever I'm around you, I feel more confident. I can't explain it. I just feel it."

My wife said, "Yeah! That's what attracted me to you. Your presence gave me confidence."

FINANCIAL FAST TRACK QUESTION

WHAT IS MY NUMBER ONE GREATEST STRENGTH?

Since that conversation, I have embraced my brand as America's #1 Confidence Coach. I have shared my message on the world's biggest stages. My books have been certified as Amazon best sellers, and my programs have helped thousands to unleash their confidence and accomplish everything God has prepared them to do.

Nobody comes into this world empty. Everyone has something unique to offer. That difference is your market differentiator. Identify it, and you can accelerate your financial achievements. Try to capture it in a single word. My word is *confidence*. John Maxwell's is *leadership*. Tony Robbins' word is *motivation*. These people are at the top of their game. They know who they are. They understand their brands.

Here's my challenge to you: Find your word. Then own your strength. That's what my 83K Academy is about. (More on this in the final chapter.)

FINANCIAL FAST TRACK FACT

YOUR DIFFERENCE WILL MAKE A DIFFERENCE. YOUR DIFFERENCE MAKES YOU EXPENSIVE.

Decision #3: Elevate Your Problems

Did you expect me to say, "Elevate your problems"? Probably not, but I said it. What I mean is, "Elevate the big problems you will solve." Wake up every morning looking for them. Become the Financial Fast Track's definition of an entrepreneur: a person who solves problems for people, organizations, or nations at a profit.

Every problem contains the seed of financial reward. Want more income? Have the confidence to pray for huge problems to solve. The size of the problem will determine the size of your reward. The supermarket cashier solves a smaller problem than the neurosurgeon does. Therefore, the cashier makes a whole lot less than the neurosurgeon's $300 per hour.

The money you need to fulfill your God-given assignment is in someone else's pocket. Even people with deep pockets have desires, needs, and problems. If you figure out how to meet their needs, they will show their appreciation by pulling some Ben Franklins from their pockets and handing them to you.

FINANCIAL FAST TRACK QUESTION

WOULD YOU RATHER SOLVE PROBLEMS FOR MILLIONS OF PEOPLE OR ONLY A FEW?

Jacob's son Joseph was a skilled interpreter of dreams. But the crux of his success was in solving other people's problems. Today we might say that Joseph became Pharaoh's second-in-command through his coaching and consulting services. But dream interpretation was his calling card. Once he helped Pharaoh understand a troubling dream, Joseph could solve the real problem which was impending famine. The consult gave Joseph tremendous influence and empowered him to establish policy at the highest levels. Because of the value he added, Egypt overcame a national and regional food shortage.

Are you working for a company? Then, solve a problem. To increase profitability, your employer must either cut costs or increase revenue. Both challenges are difficult. Bring the better solution to the table, and the firm's financial outcomes will improve. Not only will you gain influence, but you will work for a firm that can pay you more.

How do you start solving the problem? Brainstorm five ways your company can cut costs and five ways it can grow revenue. Take the best idea from each category and determine how your company can implement it. Then write down the benefits of each solution and present them to your employer.

Are you beginning to see possibility? This is how entrepreneurs think. And this is how wealth is transferred.

Decision #4: Elevate Your Expertise

Most people want their businesses to get bigger. Therefore, I challenge my coaching clients to become ten times better at what they do. I've found that if you elevate your expertise tenfold, the world will demand that your business becomes ten times bigger.

Another favorite Bible character of mine is Daniel. He lived during a difficult period of exile but leveraged his hardship by becoming highly educated in two systems: his native Hebrew culture and the system of the conquering Babylonians. The Babylonian king noticed the excellence of Daniel and his friends. Scripture says, "In all matters of wisdom and understanding about which the king examined them, he found them *ten times better* than all the magicians and astrologers who were in all his realm" (Daniel 1:20).

Daniel was a marketplace man of God who cultivated his skills and completely outshined the secular leaders around him. Therefore, the king promoted him to a top political position. Being ten times better than everyone else put Daniel on the fast track to *bigger*. But there was a specific key to his success, wealth, and influence: powerful people recognized him as an expert!

Are you adaptable to new knowledge and learning? In today's fast-paced, ever-changing business environment, you cannot overcome obstacles without embracing evolving technologies and methods. Cling to yesterday's ways, and tomorrow's successes will elude you.

You don't have to change everything in one day. But you can start today. Adapt and develop your expertise. It is easy to do using the formula that skyrocketed my income and helped me to become known as America's #1 Confidence Coach.

Are you ready for it?

R + S + 5Y = 5 Percent. Translation: **Read** (one hour per day on your) **Subject** (or field of endeavor) for **5 Years** and you will rise to the top **5 Percent** (in your field).

Want to increase your income? Great! The market will pay expert wages but only for an expert. If your income isn't where you want it to be, make sure your expertise qualifies you for more. Then go after it.

Decide today that you are becoming an expert. Make it your business to know more about your field than anybody else does. It's not hard to do, but it requires a firm decision. Make that decision, and it will make you wealthy.

FINANCIAL FAST TRACK FACT

BE A LIFELONG STUDENT. THE MORE YOU LEARN, THE MORE YOU EARN.

Decision # 5: Elevate Your Skills

My 2002 financial crisis revealed that my skill sets needed work. I had already spent ten years developing my speaking skills, but I lagged in other areas. So, I focused on developing my marketing, sales, business, strategic planning, and coaching skills.

At the time, my potential to make an impact was tremendous. Speaking around the globe and becoming a best-selling author were possible for me. I even had the potential to charge clients $120,000 to work with me. However, I had limited myself. I was moving slowly because I hadn't sufficiently elevated my value.

> ‖‖‖‖‖‖‖‖‖‖‖‖‖‖‖‖‖ **FINANCIAL FAST TRACK FACT** ‖‖‖‖‖‖‖‖‖‖‖‖‖‖‖
>
> ## POTENTIAL MUST BE TURNED INTO SKILL. SKILL INCREASES THE SPEED AND VALUE OF YOUR LABOR.

King Solomon said, "If the ax is dull, and one does not sharpen the edge, then he must use more strength; but wisdom brings success" (Ecclesiastes 10:10). The axe metaphor is powerful, but if you plan to cut down a tree, an axe is not your only option.

» You can karate chop the tree with your hand, but it probably won't work.

» You can hack away at the tree with a hammer, but it will take forever.

» You can use a dull axe, but you'll spend several hours to finish the job.

» You can use a chainsaw and have the tree down in fifteen minutes.

» Or you can break out the bulldozer and take it down in five.

Forgive the mixed metaphors, but your skills and tools are your secret sauce. The right skills increase your value in the marketplace rapidly. Upgrade your tools, and you maximize your skills and your time. The bulldozer is ideal, but the chainsaw is also effective. Upgrade your skills to at least those levels. Working harder is not the answer. Add some "smarter" to your "harder," and you'll win.

> ‖‖‖‖‖‖‖‖‖‖‖‖‖‖‖‖‖ **FINANCIAL FAST TRACK FACT** ‖‖‖‖‖‖‖‖‖‖‖‖‖‖‖
>
> ## SKILLS MULTIPLY AND ACCELERATE YOUR PRODUCTIVITY.

Monetize Your Skills

Why are multiplication and acceleration so important? It's because you cannot create (print) money. What you can do is monetize your skills, and they will generate income. Doing this requires a confident belief in your abilities and your worthiness to monetize them. Know that you *can* ask a lot of money when you offer genuine value.

So, how do you get the ball rolling toward financial increase?

» First, you must believe that you can make money by monetizing your skills.

» Then you must believe that you can monetize them further by charging more.

» You must also believe that you can store and invest money (a minimum of 10 percent of your income).

» Then you can grow and multiply your money by investing it.

» With investments working for you, you can enjoy your returns and help others.

If this concept excites you, you are probably wondering which skills you can monetize the fastest. Whatever your giftings, it is imperative that you master four primary skills: marketing, communication, coaching, and technology.

Marketing Skills

It staggers me to learn how many people don't know what business they are in. For years I would have told you I was in the speaking business. Maybe you would say that you're a chiropractor, manufacturer, painter, baker, or pastor.

Wrong! Whatever your field, you are first and foremost in the marketing business. I'm not sure when *marketing* became a dirty word. It simply means getting out your message. For example, God is in the redemption and reconciliation business. But He is love, and His message is love. He has masterfully spread (aka "marketed") that message for millennia. I don't know anyone else who can make that claim.

Throughout the Old Testament, God sent His prophets to herald the coming Savior. When the time was near, God sent John the Baptist to get out the word in the marketplace. John was a wild-looking man who drew large crowds. He prepared the way for the Son of God, first and foremost by spreading the news about Him.

Messaging hasn't changed all that much since then. You still need to master your marketing. Whatever your mission is, you need to position, package, and promote yourself. The average American is bombarded by at least four thousand advertisements per day.[65] If you don't cut through the clutter, it will bury your voice.

---

65   Ron Marshall, "How Many Ads Do You See in One Day?" *Red Crow Marketing, Inc.*, 10 Sep. 2015, https://www.redcrowmarketing.com/2015/09/10/many-ads-see-one-day/.

> |||||||||||||||||||||||||||| **FINANCIAL FAST TRACK FACT** ||||||||||||||||||||||||||||
>
> ## MARKETING MEANS GETTING ATTENTION, SO MORE PEOPLE WILL KNOW WHO YOU ARE AND WHAT YOU OFFER.

You are no longer competing with the guy down the road. The world started out flat. Then we discovered it was round. Now, it is flat again, meaning that business used to be simple and local, but the internet pitted the entire globe against you. At the same time, it opened broader fields of possibility. You are no longer constrained by time or distance. You can sell any time of the day or night, anywhere in the world, provided people know you exist. If you ignore marketing, you do it to your own detriment.

Communication Skills

When you clearly communicate your vision, share your story, and authentically connect with others, magic happens. Remember that the communications field is among the highest-paid. When you commit to growing as a communicator, you commit to growing your income. Those who master this skill can expect to earn millions.

A clearly communicated vision empowers others to come alongside and build your dream. Tell your story, and your difference can make you a fortune. Connect authentically with people and groups, and your influence will be multiplied. Ultimately, your income will reflect your impact on others.

Communication is the primary gift that makes room for you and brings you before great men and women (Proverbs 18:16). Every day, I see this playing out for my clients. Whether they are pitching their concepts in boardrooms, making high-ticket sales calls, networking with dream-makers, or speaking to the masses, communication unlocks their financial acceleration.

Coaching Skills

Today's leader needs to maximize the potential of his or her team. That means developing excellent coaching skills. Coaching is knowing how to listen so that you speak with candor and authority. Leaders who listen well add weight to their words. By listening, they learn whether a particular person responds best to softness or strength.

Culturally, we desperately need leadership. As leaders, the primary skill we must develop is our ability to coach others. If you intend to maximize your potential and influence the masses, you must coach people effectively. This is primarily an act of service, but it has rewards.

Technology Skills

To succeed in the coming decades, you must quit claiming that you are not tech savvy. "Leave that to the young people" is an excuse for future failures. It will doom you to financial disappointment.

Artificial intelligence is upon us. You cannot avoid becoming adept. *You can learn.* Don't be a Luddite. Do you know who the Luddites were? They were highly skilled textile workers who resisted the Industrial Revolution's mechanization. They lost that battle, not because they were inadequate artisans, but because they refused to embrace change.

Failing to develop your technology skills is like trying to cut down your tree with karate chops. Why would you guarantee your own failure? Why not bulldoze the tree and be done in five minutes?

Technology is created to make tasks easier. Once you get going, it's mostly intuitive. Younger people are not smarter than you. They just aren't afraid to try. Know what their secret is? YouTube! They let strangers with know-how teach them stuff. And you thought they were just watching cat videos!

Seriously. YouTube is the largest how-to library on the internet. Surely, you can access a video (and if you need help with that, ask for it). Find the how-to videos you need to ace your skills and become an expert.

FINANCIAL FAST TRACK FACT

TELL YOURSELF, I EMBRACE TECHNOLOGY AS A BLESSING FROM GOD TO HELP ME IMPROVE MY FINANCIAL POSITION.

Often, the most valuable skills are learned during the toughest times. During helicopter pilot licensing, candidates practice landing their birds without power. That sounds like a crisis to me! A crisis may have motivated you to read this book. If so, commit to your future success by developing the skills that will accelerate your journey on the Financial Fast Track.

Putting It All Together

Have you made the five crucial decisions to elevate your value? Are you beefing up your four essential skills? I hope so because we are about to put them all together. Value elevation is not about checklists but about applying a proven formula. The Value Cross Formula states that **demand + supply + excellence + multiply = $**.

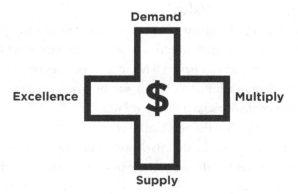

Did you know that a law governs your income? It's not a law from the government but from your mind and from the governor of the marketplace. The Law of Income says that "you will be paid in direct proportion to the value you deliver according to the marketplace."[66]

Very simply, what you are asking monetarily must align with market demand, supply, excellence, and multiplication. These factors determine what you will earn, almost to the penny. Now let's see how those factors impact your

---

66   T. Harv Eker, *Secrets of the Millionaire Mind* quoted in Seth Kniep, "How T. Harv Eker Became a Multimillionaire by Changing His Mind and How You Can Too," Just One Dime, 24 Jan. 2017, https://justonedime.com/blog/how-t-harv-eker-became-a-multimillionaire-by-changing-his-mind-and-how-you-can-too.

value. Understanding this is critical because until you offer great value, you won't get great pay.

Demand Increases Your "Value"

Have you noticed how the multitudes followed Jesus? They did it because they wanted to hear His message, receive healing, and be delivered from whatever kept them from enjoying abundance. Because Jesus offered what they wanted and needed, He was in demand.

Demand indicates how much the marketplace wants or needs what you are offering. To create demand and get on the Financial Fast Track, you must offer highly desirable, viable products or services.

Before my first speaking engagement in Asia in 2004, I learned from reports that Asians tend to lack confidence. That lack created huge demand for teachings about confidence. I will never forget what happened when I spoke there. The people purchased more than $50,000 worth of my books and training materials after one speech! I made $50,000 in three hours because my value was in high demand.

Supply Increases Your "Value"

Imagine if Jesus charged money for His miracles. I'm not suggesting that He would or should have. But what would it be worth to have your brother raised from the dead? What would you pay to have your blind eyes opened, or your only son delivered from demonic influence? Jesus was an expert where healing was concerned, and many people desperately needed Him.

So, what about supply? It is the availability of your product or service—in other words, the amount that exists in the marketplace or elsewhere. That availability determines supply. The higher the supply, the lower the price is, and vice versa.

That is why a heart surgeon earns in one day what some Wendy's employees earn in a year. The surgeon's specialized skills are in comparatively short supply and are critical when needed. To be blunt, millions are serving sandwiches, but very few people can open and repair a human heart.

FINANCIAL FAST TRACK FACT

WHEN SUPPLY IS LIMITED, VALUE INCREASES.

The same principle applies to oceanfront real estate. Properties on the water are in limited supply. Even with the US's lengthy coastlines, inland property is in far greater supply. Therefore, most homes are built there. Oceanfront homes have a much higher value because there are so few of them.

To increase your value in business, you must (1) provide what few others can provide or (2) perform in a way that few others perform. Know what your difference is, and play to it.

Excellence Increases Your "Value"

Among both friends and foes, Jesus was known for doing "all things well" (Mark 7:37). He was a man of excellence—the very best. When He preached to the multitudes, they wanted more. When He taught in the synagogues, His wit and wisdom shocked the rabbis.

To be in demand, your products, services, craft, or business must excel. That means they must reflect your never-ending, passionate pursuit of improvement. The higher the level of excellence, the greater the value of what you offer. And the greater the value, the more money will flow from it.

Excellence is becoming rare, making it even more of a wealth magnet. Why does Chick-fil-A have three lanes of drive-thru customers wrapped around their buildings? It's because their food and service are exponentially better than all their competitors' offerings combined!

I have a motto: "Do it well, or don't do it. Make it great, or don't make it at all."

Does excellence affect your income? Absolutely! Do you return to businesses that sold you shoddy goods or gave you lousy service? Of course not!

How good are you at your business? Your answer writes your story. If you want the best pay, you must be the best. Even when others believe you're the best, keep learning. Study business, study your field, and study the Financial Fast Track principles as though your life depended on them because, in many ways, it does.

‖‖‖‖‖‖‖‖‖‖‖‖‖‖ **FINANCIAL FAST TRACK FACT** ‖‖‖‖‖‖‖‖‖‖‖‖‖‖

IF YOU WANT THE BEST PAY, BE
THE BEST AT WHAT YOU DO!

Multiplying Increases Your "Value"

Jesus multiplied His efforts without wasting a moment. Early in His ministry, He chose twelve disciples to mentor. After His resurrection, those who had previously gathered in the upper room duplicated His ministry on the Day of Pentecost.

Today, there are two primary ways to multiply your efforts and value. Let's explore them both.

1) **Multiplying products:** The first way is to offer a product and add a supplemental product on the back end. Think about creating a product that aligns with your business and benefits your existing clients. Or offer someone else's product that meets your clients' needs.

    If you're a masseuse, you can offer clients products that enhance the after-massage experience and benefit overall health and well-being. Nutritional supplements, body oils, aromatherapy products, books on massage and yoga, and relaxation programs add a back-end sale to the initial transaction.

2) **Duplicating yourself:** The second way to multiply is to duplicate yourself. Develop and train others to work for you. Instead of being a solo coach or consultant, develop an agency with five, ten, or fifty coaches working for you. This method delivers more value to the market, which results in more income.

The $37,500,000 Wedding Gift

Allow me to tie together some of the concepts from this chapter with John chapter 2 as a backdrop. It is the story of Jesus' first miracle, which He performed at a wedding that He and His mother, Mary, attended. When the wine ran out, she asked Jesus to help. Although He was reluctant, Mary had a team ready to go.

Jesus instructed the team to find six ceremonial washing pots and fill them with water. Then He told them to serve a cup of that water to the master of the banquet. The master realized it was not water but wine. So, he told the bridegroom, "Usually the best wine is served at the beginning of the evening. The cheap wine is brought out after the guests are drunk and can't tell the difference. But you saved the best for last" (see John 2:10).

If you are a Christian, you probably know this story. But now look at it with our topic in mind. When Jesus showed up, there was *demand* from the wedding guests, who wanted more wine. The *supply* was limited because they had already polished off the original supply. Jesus replenished it, turning water into *excellent* wine. The marketplace (the banquet master) confirmed the wine's excellence, and it was *multiplied.* Each of six water pots now contained one hundred and fifty gallons of valuable product.

I realize that Jesus was not out to make a buck, but if you do the math with the average price of Dom Perignon as a guide, this multiplication miracle produced a potential value over $37,500,000.

That is quite a wedding gift!

The point is that you create wealth when you find demand, offer a supply, upgrade it with excellence, and multiply it for the masses. You cannot do this until you decide whether you will increase your value or join the cult of mediocrity. Raising your standards requires a commitment to maximize your strengths and solve big problems. Do both, and you will (1) become a top expert in your field and (2) make top money.

Making the five decisions described in this chapter will elevate your value and accelerate your wealth. I say this confidently because I have lived it and have seen it proven in many other lives. When I made these choices in 2002, my income doubled for three consecutive years. That is acceleration, and it is possible for you!

Want to add accelerant to your acceleration? Learn to develop Level 10 relationships, next.

. . . .

FINANCIAL FAST TRACK COACHING

1) List your thoughts about how you can elevate your value in five key areas:

   Your standards

   Your strengths

   Your problems

   Your expertise

   Your skills

2) What is your number one strength and why?

3) What skills do you need to develop to achieve faster and more excellent results?

FINANCIAL
FAST TRACK

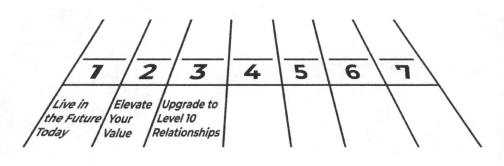

1	2	3	4	5	6	7
Live in the Future Today	Elevate Your Value	Upgrade to Level 10 Relationships				

8

LEVEL 10 RELATIONSHIPS: ESTABLISHING YOUR MILLION-DOLLAR ROUNDTABLE

You can reach a destination fast all by yourself. Case in point: When my wife and I travel from our house to Tampa International Airport, it takes us forty-five minutes. But when I jump in my Corvette all by my lonesome, I can get there in twenty-five (with my radar detector on).

I get to the airport faster on my own. But I also have some problems to confess, including one that most people don't know about. I can only drive for a couple of hours before dozing off. I've learned that if I want to go fast and far, I can't do it alone. My wife, on the other hand, can drive for eight hours without so much as a potty break (seriously).

The moral of the story is you can't go far without relationships. The right relationships—what I call Level 10 relationships—will take you further in your life, career, business, and finances than you could ever go alone, even in your 'Vette with your radar detector on.

Unexpected People Power

You've probably heard that "there are no shortcuts to success." Everybody seems to agree, and I did too. But now I believe something different because I experienced something different.

There was a knock on my mother-in-law's door. An old friend stopped by with a gift he felt impressed to give me. It was a high-quality magazine filled with pictures of the most beautiful homes in the Tampa Bay area.

With a puzzled look, I thanked him. Then he said, "Don't let your current situation convince you that your future will be the same as your present. Keep dreaming big! Look through this magazine and find the house of your dreams. Cut out the picture and put it on your refrigerator door. When you go to the fridge, look at that house and imagine yourself owning it. Then boldly say, 'I will live in this house soon!'"

Honestly, I thought he was crazy. But the next morning, Bonnie and I sat at the table and thumbed through the magazine. We allowed our imaginations to run wild, and we found our mini-mansion dream home. We figured maybe we could own one like it when we turned sixty. Yet, we followed my friend's instructions. We put the picture on the refrigerator and declared that we would live in a home like that one day.

A few months later, we visited one of the most prestigious gated communities in our area. To our amazement, we found a house that resembled the one in the picture. As we gazed in awe, I noticed a faded "For Sale" sign hidden in the bushes.

Suddenly, confidence arose in my heart, and the words of Jesus came to mind: "If you can believe, all things are possible to him who believes" (Mark 9:23). I picked up my phone and dialed the number on the sign. Acting like I had all the money in the world, I scheduled an appointment to see the house. That same day, I even agreed on a price with the owner.

Bonnie and I had only one challenge to overcome: we didn't have any money!

With just one month to get the funds, I thought we needed a financial miracle—like maybe a check arriving in our mailbox out of the blue. So, I checked every day. Nothing arrived but stacks of junk mail and bills.

One afternoon, three days before closing, I received a strange call from my office: "There's a guy who wants to have breakfast with you."

I knew who the guy was. He always wore one of those free "I gave blood" T-shirts and baggy, faded shorts. He drove a beat-up Toyota Corolla that did not impress me. When I prayed for an open door, I never imagined it would be packaged like this.

iiiiiiiiiiiiiiiiiiiiiiiiiiii **FINANCIAL FAST TRACK FACT** iiiiiiiiiiiiiiiiiiiiiiiiiiii

NEVER JUDGE THE DEPTH OF THE POCKETS BY THEIR OWNER'S OUTWARD APPEARANCE.

Over biscuits and gravy, I learned that this fellow lived in the same gated neighborhood where we made our deal. I told him I was buying a house down the street from him but needed financing. He chuckled and said, "I've been known to lend money to people to buy houses. Pick your house, and I'll lend you the money for it."

Wait—*what*! Seriously? I'm supposed to close in the next few days."

He simply said, "Just tell me the price, and my attorney will draw up the paperwork." I nearly fell off my chair.

"Don't you want to check my credit report or see my tax returns?"

"No, I've watched you over the years, and I know you're a man of character."

The money transferred to our account the day before our closing. A month later, my wife and I moved in. The dream home we thought would take years happened within months.

God opened two relationship doors to help us radically and quickly change our living arrangements and increase our wealth. Over dinner, one person coached us to dream big. Over breakfast, another financed our dream.

iiiiiiiiiiiiiiiiiiiiiiiiiiii **FINANCIAL FAST TRACK FACT** iiiiiiiiiiiiiiiiiiiiiiiiiiii

THERE IS A SHORTCUT TO CREATING WEALTH AND LIVING YOUR DREAMS—RELATIONSHIPS!

Relationships, Influence, and Impact

The quality of your relational network determines the level of your impact on a wide range of people. I was teaching on this subject when a young, struggling couple approached me. Oozing contempt, the male partner said, "Getting wealthy is all about whom you know."

"Yes!" I replied. "And the quicker you understand that the faster your life will change. Don't be angry that relationship wealth is essential to your success. Become someone who can attract divine connections."

Here's a thought for singles: set a goal to marry up, financially speaking. The current trend involves successful women marrying men for whom they must provide. These women are marrying down.

That is not what Naomi encouraged Ruth to do. She pointed her daughter-in-law to the financial fast track of their day. She instructed Ruth to be seen—not by someone who needed her paycheck but by a very good and rich man named Boaz.

Naomi showed Ruth how to marry up by going up. If she wanted a man like Boaz to notice her, she needed to improve herself. So, Ruth put on her finest dress and some perfume. You need money to dress well and look good for the right people! Many singles want Level 10 partners but don't become Level 10 candidates. (Level 5 people rarely attract Level 10 relationships.)

King Solomon knew how to leverage relationships. He married an Egyptian princess to ensure a strategic partnership with Pharaoh (1 Kings 3:1). I'm not suggesting that you marry the "wrong" person to create the "right" financial picture. I am encouraging you to leverage your relationships. It is a proven shortcut to success, freedom, and acceleration.

FINANCIAL FAST TRACK FACT

RELATIONSHIPS ARE YOUR GREATEST LEVERAGE.

During the COVID-19 pandemic, Bonnie and I were able to build and move into our current dream home. A new moving company got us packed up and settled in our new place. They did such a great job that I asked the owner for some business cards, so I could recommend the company. He was grateful but said he was limited to local moves because he could not afford a larger truck.

The coach in me couldn't be still. I said, "You aren't limited by resources. You're limited by relationships. Develop a relationship with a bigger company in our city who can move people across state lines. The next time you get an interstate inquiry, commit to the client and partner with the bigger company to get the job done."

He called me a week later to say that he referred an out-of-state opportunity to another company. The other firm gave him a commission on the move, plus two local jobs. Imagine the opportunities that can come from leveraging your strategic partnerships!

Part of that leverage comes from understanding the Law of Association. Abraham was Lot's wealthy, favored uncle. Lot was not the wisest character, but he was smart enough to stick with Abraham for an extended season. The Law of Association says that you become the people with whom you spend the most time. So, guess what happened when Lot stuck with wealthy Abraham? You guessed it! He got rich (Genesis 13:5–6).

To become a millionaire, you had better associate with multimillionaires. To become a multimillionaire, you must create strategic partnerships with billionaires.

FINANCIAL FAST TRACK FACT

WHEN GOD WANTS TO BLESS YOU, HE BRINGS THE RIGHT PERSON INTO YOUR LIFE. WHEN THE ENEMY WANTS TO DESTROY YOU, HE BRINGS THE WRONG PERSON INTO YOUR LIFE. DISCERNMENT TELLS THE DIFFERENCE!

Level 10 Relationships Accelerate Your Dreams

A big dream of mine was to penetrate the secular marketplace with my writings. I knew that to impact a broad audience, I needed a large, New York publisher to accept my manuscript. However, without celebrity, attracting such a publisher would take a miracle.

While attending a conference, I overcame my fears and invited a famous, million-plus best-selling author to dinner. I didn't take him to the Golden Corral. I did it right. I wasn't buying a meal; I was making an investment.

Apparently, my confidence was contagious. Without even knowing me, the man accepted my invitation, and we developed a relationship over dinner. He listened as I explained my publishing dream. That night, he connected me with a New York agent who helped me land an advance with Penguin Books (currently number one in the top five trade publishers). It was a miracle—over the dinner table!

FINANCIAL FAST TRACK FACT

I ALWAYS PAY FOR DINNER WHEN I'M WITH HIGHLY SUCCESSFUL LEADERS. PAY ANY PRICE TO BE IN THE PRESENCE OF GREATNESS. WHEN THEY KNOW YOU'LL PAY, YOU'LL GET MORE INVITES. A $200 DINNER IS BETTER THAN A $20,000 COACHING BILL.

My next big dream was to speak at the largest business seminar company in the world. This dream was accomplished through my relationship with a local small-church pastor. Over dinner, he connected me with the seminar company's CEO. During lunch at one of my favorite beachfront restaurants, that CEO and I forged a friendship, and he asked me to join the tour.

That CEO recently informed me that during the past year, I spoke to more than 100,000 entrepreneurs and business leaders, just through his seminar company. Once again, I learned not to judge the opportunity by what I see. Seemingly small hinges (like that small-church pastor) can open big doors.

You might be thinking, "Okay, I get it. Some incredible things have happened through your relationships. But what makes you think they can happen to me?"

My answer is simple: "Become intentional about forming Level 10 Relationships." If you do that, what happened to me can happen to you.

The power of the Level 10 relationship is its high value exchange. One of my Level 10 relationships is a world-renowned motivational speaker. He has been a New York Times best-selling author and has spoken before the largest audiences on the planet. Through that relationship I have learned to be a better storyteller. I've also learned the importance of writing a flagship book for each message that I share. The relationship is not one-sided, however. Through our exchange, my associate has improved his marketing skills and is more open to new technologies for building his client list and converting more sales.

Level 10 Relationships are about associating with people who have been where you desire to go. No one has all the answers, so Level-10 relationships are mutually beneficial.

Your Dream 20 List

Shortly after Bonnie and I purchased our first dream home, I came up with a concept similar to Level 10 Relationships, but with a client-centric approach. Remember when I hung that picture of our ideal home on the refrigerator? Well, I decided to write down the names of twenty people with whom I most wanted client relationships. I called it my Dream 20 list. It consisted of people who seemed out of my reach, yet I believed I could help them to achieve massive results.

The idea is to aim for "big game." If I were advising hunters, I would say, "Don't go rabbit hunting. Look for elephants!" If I were talking to people who love fishing, I'd say, "Don't go after minnow. Catch yourself a marlin."

That's the Dream 20 idea. Within ten years of creating my list, everyone on it became a close friend and personal client. If I were at liberty to share their identities, you would recognize them as household names. I know them because I owned my desire to have them as clients. Then, I acted according to my desire.

There is a reward for setting your intentions and then bringing value to people of power. Proverbs 22:29 says that people who excel in their work will stand before great men and women. My Dream 20 list has done that for me. I encourage you to try it.

The Level 10 Process

Your Level 10 relationships involve successful people who do what you want to do, have what you want to have, or help the people you want to help. They become exemplars and allies who help you reach your desired destination. It is an "iron sharpening iron" dynamic in which everybody wins (Proverbs 27:17).

Obviously, establishing these alliances is a process. The following five steps have worked for me. They will work for you too.

Step 1: Establish Your Table

The table is always a special place to gather. We gather with loved ones in everyday life and for holidays and special events. We reserve a table for a romantic dinner with our significant other. We catch up with friends and neighbors over the picnic table and some summer barbecue. The table is a place of relationship where quality conversations flow easily.

Your million-dollar roundtable serves a similar purpose. You create a table of people who surround you with support. It is an "invitation only" relationship, and you choose from trusted people in your inner circle. You give them your ear, and they give you theirs. You influence each other's thinking, behavior, and even the direction of your lives.

The size of your roundtable is important. You can only handle a certain number of relationships effectively. Once the table is full, it's full. You're not looking for quantity but meaningful interaction. Therefore, your seating choices must be deliberate. Every so often, you reflect on who is sitting at your table and decide whether they have been positive additions. If not, you make changes by reaching out to others. The process of building a better roundtable is ongoing.

Step 2: Evaluate Your Table

Living in my mother-in-law's house forced me to evaluate my relationships and ask this tough question: who's sitting at my table, and why?

I discovered that my table included people who didn't want me to grow, did not value my dreams, and were not helping me. In fact, some friends and family members were hurting me. I had to answer for why they were still in my inner circle. I'm not talking here about choosing your family members. I'm talking about establishing your roundtable.

Learn to detect the "scent" of your table. Have you ever noticed an obnoxious odor but become "nose blind" to it? This can happen with the people who sit at your table. After a while, you adapt to their negative ways. You learn to think like them, and you adopt their habits.

FINANCIAL FAST TRACK FACT

INFLUENCE IS POWERFUL BUT SUBTLE. IF YOU LINGER AT A GARBAGE HEAP, YOU WILL ABSORB ITS ODOR AND BE NONE THE WISER.

Each of us must evaluate our inner circle and carefully fill the seats at our table. It can be painful to weed out those who no longer belong there. But we must do it. Either they go, or we go nowhere. So, let me coach you through a process of evaluating your roundtable using my Level 10 Relationship Questionnaire:

» What kinds of people are sitting at my table?
» Where are they going in life?
» Are they successful?
» What are they doing for me?
» Are we challenging each other to grow or to stay the same?
» Do they inspire me to read books? What kinds of books?
» Do they have the wisdom to help me achieve my assignment?
» What do their financial blueprints look like?

The seats at your roundtable are invaluable. You are accountable for using them wisely. Your evaluation process will often lead to tough decisions. That's okay. It is part of telling yourself and others the truth. It is part of growing.

Step 3: Clear Your Table

Back when I first wanted to be a best-selling author, I didn't know many authors, much less best-selling ones. I wanted to be a millionaire but didn't have any millionaire friends. I wanted to be an internationally known leadership coach, but I didn't have a successful leadership coach of my own.

None of the people in my life had achieved what I wanted for my future. Therefore, they couldn't help me get there. To change my life, I had to disconnect from them and connect with the people God had for me.

FINANCIAL FAST TRACK FACT

THINK OF YOURSELF AS AN ELEVATOR. ON YOUR WAY TO YOUR DESTINATION (THE TOP), YOU MIGHT HAVE TO STOP AND LET SOME PEOPLE GET OFF.

One wrong relationship can kill your momentum. One Jonah on your boat can bring storms crashing down on you (Jonah 1:3–15). The people who sailed with Jonah were innocent. But because they allowed him to travel with them, they caught his grief. Finally, they had to kick him off. That's when the storms stopped.

According to the Law of Replacement, you need to replace what does not serve your goals. When you lose one person from your life or team, you can attract someone better. But you must patiently pursue someone with more wisdom, skills, or talents. Until you release one, you cannot add the other. And until you replace the people who no longer fit, you cannot achieve the increase that would otherwise be possible.

This process will test your confidence. Trust me! It's not easy to leave the relationships at your table. Reaching for new, bigger, and better ones takes a level of confidence that "comfortable" relationships don't require. Those old alliances make you feel safe and secure without challenging you or demanding you to think differently. They simply accept you "as is" because they are on or below your level. They may be your friends, but they are the enemy of your potential.

> *My **best** friend is the one who brings out the **best** in me.*[67]
> —Henry Ford

Step 4: Upgrade Your Table

Creating a new, confident, and competent table of Level 10 relationships requires vigilance. What you want and need at your table are moral, successful, wealthy, and confident people who believe in you and your vision for the future. If anyone at your table does not match that description, they are not your roundtable.

Choose friendships that build, support, and reinforce your character, competence, and confidence on the Financial Fast Track. Be selective. Your orbit will always include confidence-shakers and confidence-makers. The former will release words that discourage you. They always see something negative in what you seek to accomplish. That doesn't mean you surround yourself with panderers. It means you surround yourself with people who can be frank but genuinely supportive.

FINANCIAL FAST TRACK FACT

COMPETENCE: THE ABILITY TO DO SOMETHING. CONFIDENCE: YOUR BELIEF ABOUT YOUR COMPETENCE.

---

67 "Henry Ford > Quotes > Quotable Quote," *Goodreads*, accessed September 30, 2021, https://www.goodreads.com/quotes/34931-my-best-friend-is-the-one-who-brings-out-the.

You will find that the most supportive people are those who are not threatened by your dreams. Why? Because they are competent, wealthy, and successful. You'll need confidence to connect with them, but that is part of the process. You improve your game by playing with better players who can spur you to go higher. Yes, it can be intimidating at first. But it is a major key to increasing your competence and confidence.

What about your family members? Who is the wealthiest and most successful person in your family? My grandfather ran a very successful insulation company in our city. There was only one problem—everybody in the family hated him. Why? Because he wouldn't use his money to bail them out of their stupidity. Sadly, when I could have learned from him, I envied his success instead. I could easily have sought him out, but I kept my distance.

> *I have never had a hater who is doing better than me.*[68]
> —BISHOP T. D. JAKES

The greatest gift anyone can give you is access. I had open access to my grandfather but didn't use it. When successful people give you their time, don't take it lightly. Give *them* as much of your time as possible. Don't forget to thank them for the time they give you. When a person is grateful for my time, I reward them with more of it.

Step 5: Assign Seating at Your Table

When I think about the people I want at my table, Joseph comes to mind. Remember: his greatest skill was problem-solving. We've already seen how he helped Pharaoh prepare for famine, but Pharaoh was not his first client. Joseph helped some others before Pharaoh summoned him:

1) Potiphar—Joseph caused Potiphar's house and fields to prosper.

2) The prison warden—Joseph was put in charge, and the prison prospered.

3) Pharaoh's butler—Joseph interpreted his dream.

4) Pharaoh's baker—Joseph interpreted his dream.

5) Pharaoh—Joseph interpreted his dream and formed policy.

6) Joseph's family—Joseph saved them from famine and economic disaster.

7) Egypt—Joseph saved the nation from starvation.

---

68 T. D. Jakes (@BishopJakes), "I've never had a hater who was doing better than me," Twitter, September 4, 2015, 11:27 p.m., https://twitter.com/bishopjakes/status/640003229212782592?lang=en.

Every problem Joseph solved increased his influence and ultimately solved his own wealth problem (Genesis 39–41). To go from the pit to the palace, he needed these influential connections. By serving, he became known to Pharaoh.

||||||||||||||||||||||||| **FINANCIAL FAST TRACK FACT** |||||||||||||||||||||||||

MONEY IS NEITHER A MIRACLE NOR A MYSTERY. MONEY IS SIMPLY A REWARD FOR SOLVING PROBLEMS AND MEETING THE NEEDS OF OTHERS. BIG PROBLEMS MEAN BIG REWARDS. RUN CONFIDENTLY TOWARD THEM.

Of all the people Joseph helped, three were essential to his roundtable: the baker, the butler, and Pharaoh.

The Baker

Bakers always have the recipes and pull together the ingredients. Often, we have the raw goods our assignments require, but we haven't learned to combine them. In other words, we don't know the recipe. Raw talent is great, but it's like raw flour—no one wants to eat it! But when the ingredients are properly blended and baked, everyone wants what comes out of the oven. That's the baker's job: bringing together the raw ingredients with a recipe to manifest your dreams. You need a baker at your table.

The Butler

Butlers open new doors. One night, after I dined at an extravagant restaurant, the valet asked for the ticket for my Mercedes. Moments later, he arrived with a gorgeous Rolls-Royce Wraith. He hopped out of the car and said, "Here you are, Dr. Johnson."

I thought, "Hallelujah! The butler hath opened unto me a new door!"

We had a good laugh about the mix-up. But you get my point. The right butler is a connector who can open the right doors and lead you from your familiar places into brand-new, amazing relationships. Make sure you have a butler seated at your table.

Pharaoh (Joseph's Mentor)

When Joseph came into relationship with Pharaoh, both men's fortunes changed. But for Joseph, *everything* changed. When you're praying for a miracle, you might find a mentor who will help you fast-track your life, business, and finances. He or she can teach you how to shorten your learning curve and expedite your increase.

As King Solomon said, "He who walks with wise men will be wise, but the companion of fools will be destroyed" (Proverbs 13:20). It was obvious to many that Joseph was destined for the throne. But he could not get there without the help of a king. That help came when Pharaoh requested his presence.

Make room at your table for the baker, the butler, and Pharaoh. Seek wise people, and they will make you wealthy. Avoid fools. They will destroy your dreams. Begin investing in Level 10 relationships. They might teach you their secrets—like how to own and pay yourself first.

⊪⊪⊪⊪⊪⊪⊪⊪⊪⊪ FINANCIAL FAST TRACK FACT ⊪⊪⊪⊪⊪⊪⊪⊪⊪⊪

PEOPLE ARE LIKE DOORS. THEY HELP YOU MOVE FROM ONE SEASON TO ANOTHER, ONE LEVEL TO ANOTHER, AND ONE RELATIONSHIP TO ANOTHER.

. . . .

FINANCIAL FAST TRACK COACHING

Let's get down to cases. These exercises are keys to your future, so consider them carefully and follow through. It is not enough to write down your answers. You need to act on what you know. Until you do, nothing changes!

1) Evaluate those who are currently seated at your table. Write down their names and describe each person's role and effect on your life.

1. _____

2. _____

3. _____

4. _____

5. _____

6. _____

7. _____

8. _____

9. _____

10. _____

2) Which people should you exclude from your table going forward? Write down their names and make your moves.

3) Make your Dream 20 relationship list. These are the people with whom you want to connect in the future.

1. _____

2. _____

3. _____

4. _____

5. _____

6. _____

7. _____

8. _____

9. _____

10. _____

11. _____

12. _____

13. _____

14. _____

15. _____

16. _____

17. _____

18. _____

19. _____

20. _____

Well done! But remember that nothing changes until you act. The real power is in what you do next.

FINANCIAL
FAST TRACK

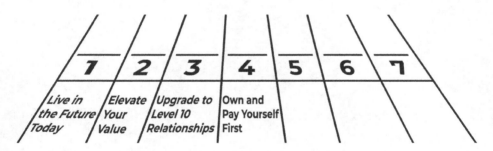

1	2	3	4	5	6	7
Live in the Future Today	Elevate Your Value	Upgrade to Level 10 Relationships	Own and Pay Yourself First			

9

OWNING AND PAYING YOURSELF FIRST: EXPAND YOUR OPPORTUNITY FUND TO BECOME AN INVESTOR

Pay your bills first, and if you have money left over, save it for a rainy day." That was the financial advice I absorbed from my parents, teachers, preachers, and society at large. It was conventional wisdom, and most people followed it. The fact that very few of them were wealthy should have been a red flag.

I learned what the problem was when one of my millionaire mentors asked me an eye-opening question: "If an investment opportunity came your way, how's your liquidity?"

Ashamed, I responded, "Two hundred and thirty-three dollars." Laughing, I added, "That's more than I started with."

He said, "There's hope for you, but you have to start loving yourself more."

I thought, *What's love got to do with becoming a millionaire?*

||||||||||||||||||||||||| **FINANCIAL FAST TRACK FACT** |||||||||||||||||||||||||

YOUR SELF-WORTH WILL ULTIMATELY DETERMINE YOUR NET WORTH.

Then he asked this strange question: "Do you pay your bills as soon as you get your paycheck?"

In almost ignorant confidence, I answered, "Yes! I pay all my bills first. And, praise God, I have never been late!"

Then he dropped a financial bomb. "Keith, you need to *stop* paying your bills first."

My mind went on tilt. *What?* Then I thought, *This guy is crazy!* Instantly, I reconsidered. *But he's really rich, and I'm not, so I had better listen up.* When I caught my breath, I voiced a logical concern: "I am struggling from month to month to pay my bills. If I pay myself before my bills, some of them won't get paid. I'll have to miss a car payment, an electric bill, or the rent. Then what?"

That's when my Financial Fast Track education caught fire. He said, "You are thinking like poor and middle-class people who don't love themselves. That isn't how the rich think or behave. If you will start thinking opposite to your conditioning, you will discover how wealthy people think about finances. They think the way they do because they love themselves."

It was a lightbulb moment. The rich honor their self-worth. Therefore, they value themselves and their time. Their self-worth is so high that they refuse to trade their time for money. The rich believe in *owning themselves first.* That means they are in control of starting, growing, and scaling their businesses (more on applying this in Financial Fast Track #7). They expect to be paid first for their hard work because they believe they deserve it.

============================== **FINANCIAL FAST TRACK FACT** ==============================

OWN AND PAY YOURSELF FIRST.
THEN PAY YOUR BILLS.

The poor and middle class have been taught the opposite of what the rich believe. Therefore, their sense of self-worth tends to be lower, and they undervalue their time. Subconsciously, they don't believe they deserve to own and pay themselves first. They think everyone else deserves the first cut. Sadly, they rarely have any money left at the end of the month, so they don't pay themselves at all. They just stay broke and make other people rich.

For the rich, money rarely runs short. But if it does, they make everyone else wait to get paid. Strangely enough, when you practice this principle, you always have enough to pay your monthly bills. How that works is a mystery, so don't try to figure it out. Just remember that success leaves clues. Do what rich and successful people do, and you will get rich and successful results.

I admit that the concept my mentor shared blew me away. During the long drive home, I wondered, *How am I going to explain this to my wife? She takes care of the bills. I don't think she'll want to change our financial habits like this.* Bonnie agreed, however, and we followed my mentor's lead. We paid ourselves before our bills, but we did not change our "God first" philosophy. We continued giving 10 percent of our income to God, as I have taught in my book *PoTENtial: The Secret Power of Ten*. Tithing is a principle historically used by billionaires like John D. Rockefeller, Henry Ford, Oprah Winfrey, and many other people of wealth.

I like to refer to tithing as "going into business with God." Bear in mind, however, that if you get the tithe right but mishandle the remaining 90 percent of your income, you will stay broke.

FINANCIAL FAST TRACK FACT

I TITHE BECAUSE I AM WISE ENOUGH TO UNDERSTAND THAT GOD KNOWS WHERE THE GOLD IS.

From Emergency Fund to Storehouse

The idea of paying ourselves before our bills was challenging because I wanted the math to make sense. I got over it, however, because my liquidity problem didn't make sense either. How could I have worked so hard for fifteen years and have only $233 to show for it?

What my mentor revealed also changed my "saving for a rainy day" strategy. I told you how that worked out: the more dollars I saved for emergencies, the more emergencies I experienced. So, I stopped saving for emergencies and started *storing* for future opportunities.

Gradually, I created liquidity that positioned me to make investments, which multiplied the money I had. I started thinking like an investor instead of a saver.

Investors aren't looking for the next crisis. They are looking for the next opportunity to invest. They don't play financial defense. They play offense and position themselves to score financial touchdowns.

They are onto something. Despite endless teachings on saving $1,000 for emergencies, most people haven't saved $500, much less $1,000. I think it's because the goal is too small. Big, life-changing goals get us off our butts and motivate us to act. Small goals cannot inspire massive action. A $1,000 emergency fund is not a life-changing achievement—not even close!

FINANCIAL FAST TRACK GOAL

SET YOUR FIRST GOAL TO STORE $100,000.

In general, it takes about $100,000 to invest in an asset that produces passive income. That asset might be a business (whether you start it, buy it, or become a franchisee) or a down payment on some real estate. When I faced my financial crisis, I bypassed the conventional $1,000 goal (which suddenly seemed tiny) and set a $100,000 goal that would be life-altering.

How did it feel to have $100,000 in the bank? I can't fully explain it, but I still remember the experience. Hitting that first storehouse goal sent my financial confidence sky high. I felt like a different person. More importantly, I believed that I could easily repeat the process until I reached and exceeded my larger $1 million goal.

My shift from an emergency fund to an opportunity fund was a big part of leaving the wealth-in-a-wheelchair philosophy. God promised to bless my storehouses, not my storm fund. There is a vast difference between the two.

FINANCIAL FAST TRACK FACT

WHEN YOU STORE FOR OPPORTUNITIES, YOU ATTRACT AN OPPORTUNITY HARVEST.

For one thing, the Bible admonishes us to maintain storehouses of food, money, and possessions. Deuteronomy 28:8 says, "The LORD will command the blessing on you in your *storehouses* and in all to which you set your hand, and He will bless you in the land which the LORD your God is giving you."

In biblical days, a storehouse was a kind of barn for storing surplus food and resources. Your storehouse doesn't have to be a physical structure, however. My first storehouse was a shoebox. Whenever I cashed a check, I put 10 percent of it in my shoebox. If someone gave me money for a birthday, Christmas, or side gig, I stored it in my shoebox. Every time I added money to my storehouse, I prayed over it and declared that my shoebox would overflow.

Eventually, I became more excited about storing money than I was about spending it. The passing pleasures of "new stuff" no longer mattered. My future mattered much more.

FINANCIAL FAST TRACK FACT

FINANCIAL MATURITY BEGINS WHEN YOUR DESIRE TO STORE RESOURCES BECOMES GREATER THAN YOUR DESIRE TO SPEND THEM.

Guess what happened? My little shoebox eventually overflowed with the second most beautiful thing on the planet: one hundred-dollar bills (the first most beautiful thing is my wife). From my shoebox storehouse, I moved to a safe deposit box at a bank. All of it was part of establishing a new lifestyle, and it paid off! My storehouse grew, and every bill was paid on time.

Storehouses and kingdom economics were subjects Joseph understood. What he shared with Pharaoh saved nations. He showed Egypt how to pay itself by storing grain during the seven years of plenty. The nation's storehouses sustained Egypt and some of its neighbors during the seven years of famine that followed. Egypt prospered while those who were unprepared starved.

Not only that, but the principle of storing goods and selling them when demand was high made Pharaoh wealthier than ever. Joseph's method provided massive opportunities for Pharaoh to acquire land, farms, and businesses. Within fourteen years, he legally owned everything in Egypt.

The principles Joseph followed are the same ones Jewish children still learn about the importance of storing and investing to become wealthy. This becomes part of their lifestyle. Yet, first-generation Jewish Christians in the Jerusalem church pooled their resources. I question that strategy because they ended up in poverty. We know this because the apostle Paul had to raise money for them (1 Corinthians 16:1–4; 2 Corinthians 8:1–9; Romans 15:14–32).

I believe their failure to create storehouses was a costly lapse in financial intelligence. Sadly, most of today's Christians are no better off. They have little or no understanding of storehouses. Therefore, they store very little, a practice that leads to having very little of anything later.

Many people say, "Your advice about storing sounds well and good, but opportunities never come to me."

Okay. Here's my question for you: "Why would God send you a million-dollar opportunity if He knows you don't have $100,000 to invest?"

You will find that when you practice the strategy I describe, opportunities will track you down. Soon, you'll have to pray for wisdom to know which opportunities to take and which to let go!

When Opportunity Comes, Pull the Trigger

Bonnie and I sat poolside at the Bahamas' Atlantis Hotel, gazing at the turquoise water and watching the palm trees wave in the breeze. I had been looking for some land in Florida where we could build a new home. Then a listing for a 1.5-acre property popped up on my iPhone.

The plot was on a very popular street in our area where all the "mansions" are. I had been eyeing that road for some time and knew the opportunity wouldn't last long. I quickly texted my real estate agent and bought the property out of my "opportunity storehouse"—all while sunbathing in the Bahamas.

Afterward, I set my sights on an adjacent five-acre lot and searched the records to find its owner. When I expressed my interest in buying the lot, she wasn't interested in selling. Then COVID-19 hit, and she was ready to sell. I dipped into my opportunity storehouse and paid the $99,000 asking price for land that was worth no less than $250,000 and had a potential future value beyond seven figures.

Here is what I find interesting: I visited two houses on the same beautiful road. By any definition, they are mansions. Guess what both owners had in common? Storehouses! Each had a bedroom-sized vault hidden behind a secret door. One owner took me inside his vault which was crammed full of cash, coins, gold, silver, and expensive collector guns. Of course, there was also a state-of-the-art security system monitoring the entire property.

My point is that paying yourself is a must, and paying yourself 10 percent is just the beginning. As your financial situation improves, your storehouse-filling capacity expands. The ultimate goal is to store as much as 40 percent of your income.

If hearing this doesn't ignite your sense of urgency, I don't know what will. But if it does, you will surely ask yourself the question below.

FINANCIAL FAST TRACK QUESTION

"HOW QUICKLY CAN I REACH THE PLACE OF STORING BETWEEN 10 AND 40 PERCENT OF MY INCOME?"

Watch Your Timing

King Solomon, the fifth wealthiest man in history said, "To everything there is a season, a time for every purpose under heaven . . . a time to gain, and a time to lose; a time to keep, and a time to throw away" (Ecclesiastes 3:1, 6).

Timing is important when you purchase dreamy liabilities like exotic cars, fancy homes, Louis Vuitton Keepalls, and Richard Mille watches. Let me explain. On July 7, 2007, my speaking and coaching business was booming. The housing market crash was about to hit, and I wanted to buy a black-on-black Mercedes SUV like one of my mentors had. Before I finalized the purchase, I told my mentor what I considered doing.

His reply ticked me off. He said, "Keith, don't buy it. If you can afford a Mercedes, then buy a Cadillac. If you can afford a Cadillac, buy a Buick. It's the same with real estate. If you can afford a $300,000 house, buy a $200,000 house instead. It will allow you to build your war chest and become a giver and investor instead of a consumer. Don't trade your dreams for nice things. When you can afford a Bentley, you're ready for your Mercedes. When you can afford the $500,000 house, go ahead and jump into the $300,000 one." (In chapter 11, I will teach you how to turn your house into a money generator instead of a liability.)

I didn't like what he said, but I knew he was right. I reluctantly bought a 2008 Cadillac DTS, drove it for twelve years, and treated it like it was my Mercedes. With more than one hundred thousand miles on it, I traded it in and purchased my black-on-black Mercedes 550S with the AMG package. I paid for that car from one of the income streams I had built over the prior decade.

When it comes to purchasing liabilities, patience is a virtue. Build your dream business first. Buy your toys later.

FINANCIAL FAST TRACK FACT

STORE RESOURCES IN YOUR OPPORTUNITY BARN. WHEN THE TIMING IS RIGHT, EMPTY THE BARN INTO AN ASSET-PRODUCING VEHICLE.

When Saving Equals Losing

Storing is a wise practice, but Jesus warned that saving money and hoarding resources can make you a loser (Matthew 6:19). Why? Because moths, rust, thieves, and inflation eventually diminish their value.

Money is called *currency*. Like a current in a stream, it must keep moving. Recessions and depressions don't happen because money is lacking. They happen because money stops moving. The stream becomes stagnant, like a swamp.

If saving is your only strategy, it's not enough. Just ask my dog. She's a lovable loser. When I give her a treat, she buries it. She thinks she's storing treasures for later, but I always find them and either trash them or return them to the treat container. She's trying to save, but she's continually losing.

That is pretty much what happens to the money you hide in your underwear drawer. The more money the government prints, the less value it has. Therefore, even as your stash seems to grow, its buying power disappears. You thought you were saving money for later, but inflation is devouring it.

The parable of the talents is a classic illustration (Matthew 25:14–30). A man of means gave his "good" servant five talents, which he invested and doubled. But another servant did what my dog does: he buried the talent. He had the mentality of a saver rather than a multiplier. The man who gave him the talent said he was "wicked and slothful" for handling money so poorly.

The story also disproves the Robin Hood philosophy of taking from the rich and giving to the poor. That is not a kingdom concept. God says, "To everyone who has will more be given, and he will have an *abundance*. But from the one who [doesn't have], even what he has will be taken away" (Matthew 25:29).

⫼⫼⫼ FINANCIAL FAST TRACK WEALTH CREATION CYCLE ⫼⫼⫼

WORK SIX DAYS > STORE IN THE BARN > EMPTY THE BARN INTO AN OPPORTUNITY > REFILL THE BARN > EMPTY THE BARN AGAIN > REFILL THE BARN AGAIN > MULTIPLY ASSETS FOR CASH FLOW.

Success leaves clues. Therefore, we should study it. Consider the behavior of Elon Musk, one of the richest men in the world. By using the Fast Track Wealth Creation Cycle, he keeps his streams flowing. That's how he became a centibillionaire.

Musk worked hard to build an online banking empire which later merged with another firm to become PayPal. Later, he filled his barn by selling PayPal for $1.5 billion,[69] $180 million of which was his.[70] Then Musk emptied his barn by developing two more barns called Tesla and SpaceX. Musk went from having $180 million on hand to borrowing food and rent money from family and friends![71]

The concept of filling your barn and then going broke by investing into another asset is a way of multiplying your wealth and protecting you from yourself. Once you know that you can fill a storehouse, you know you can empty it and fill it again.

---

69   Margaret Kane, "Ebay Picks up PayPal for $1.5 Billion," *CNET*, 18 Aug. 2002, https://www.cnet.com/news/ebay-picks-up-paypal-for-1-5-billion/.

70   Avijeet Sachdev, "Elon Musk: A Self-Made Entrepreneur," *HuffPost*, last updated February 2, 2013, https://www.huffpost.com/entry/elon-musk-a-selfmade-entr_b_2214268.

71   Sachdev, "Elon Musk . . . "

A Word of Wisdom to My Younger Self—Begin as an Investor

One of my favorite movies is *Back to School*, starring Rodney Dangerfield. In a hilarious commencement speech, Dangerfield advises the graduates to stay at home as long as they can because "It's a jungle out there!"[72]

If you are in your twenties, this is more than a funny line; it's a smart strategy for the fast track. Staying at home will enable you to store cash, start your business, and use your 40 percent storehouse to buy assets that generate cash flow. You could own an investment house or buy a business long before you move out of your parents' home!

If you are in your thirties, forties, or fifties and have experienced a major financial setback from a divorce or bankruptcy, I have similar advice: swallow your pride and move in with your parents or other caring relatives. Use that time to regroup and start storing.

A word of caution, however: keep your storehouse to yourself. Some family members will use one crisis after another to empty your barn. Bailing them out will only keep you broke. Their crises are not your crises, and your barn is not their barn. You can't help anyone (not even yourself) if you never get on your feet.

The Seasons of Money—Spring, Summer, Fall, and Winter

Can you learn from a bug? I'll let Solomon answer that question:

> *You lazy fool, look at an ant. Watch it closely; let it teach you a thing or two. Nobody has to tell it what to do. All summer it stores up food; at harvest it stockpiles provisions.* —*Proverbs 6:6–8 (MSG)*

Ants never quit. In summertime, we like to kick back, but ants keep filling up their barns. (No wonder they always seem to be in a hurry!) They teach us that you cannot chillax all summer long. Think ahead. Remember the tough times when everything looks positive, and remember the good times when winter comes. Blue skies won't always be blue. Storms will come and go. Every garden has a snake, and weeds are sure to grow.

---

72 *Back to School*, Orion Pictures, 1986. "Rodney Dangerfield—Back to School," *YouTube*, film clip, accessed October 1, 2021, https://www.youtube.com/watch?v=LF0MilNDV1I.

FINANCIAL FAST TRACK FACT

THINK LIKE THE RICH. WHEN THE ECONOMY BOOMS, IT'S TIME TO SELL. WHEN THE ECONOMY STALLS, IT'S TIME TO BUY.

The rich are like ants: they store up during summer and buy in winter. The poor and middle classes do the opposite: they buy when prices are inflated and sell to the rich when prices fall. When winter comes to their finances, they are unprepared and forced to make poor financial decisions.

Watch the ant closely! Its wisdom is the wisdom of the wealthy. Follow its lead. Own and pay yourself first, and store up for a future opportunity. Then, watch what God turn your stream into a lake of wealth!

. . . .

FINANCIAL FAST TRACK COACHING

Take your first step toward becoming an investor by establishing your storehouse. Open a bank account, or get a shoebox. But whatever you do, start storing money for your next big opportunity.

1) What next step must you take to own and pay yourself first? Exactly what will that look like for you?

2) Which "toy" purchases can you defer as you focus on building your business and your future? What substitutions can you make to help strengthen your future liquidity and viability? (Remember the example of the Cadillac versus the Mercedes.)

FINANCIAL
FAST TRACK

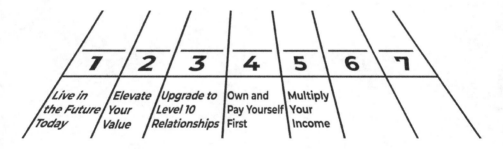

1	2	3	4	5	6	7
Live in the Future Today	Elevate Your Value	Upgrade to Level 10 Relationships	Own and Pay Yourself First	Multiply Your Income		

10

MULTIPLY YOUR INCOME AND BUILD A LAKE OF WEALTH

t's time for me to fess up. My lack of knowledge about multiplying my income contributed to the greatest financial crash of my life. The burden I carried as a father and husband was more than I could handle. The stress and humiliation of being buried in bad debt left me so low emotionally that I considered taking my life.

Yet there was hope! All of us are one right strategy away from a personal breakthrough. Discovering my Financial Fast Track was that strategy for me. It not only saved me from three major crises, but it enabled me to thrive while many in my industry crashed and burned, and some never fully recovered.

The idea of multiplying my income became my life raft during a stormy decade. It rescued me when the housing market crashed in 2007. It saved me when an emergency quintuple bypass sidelined me for about a year. It also protected me during COVID-19, when both the church and marketplace faced mandatory shutdowns. A year's worth of my speaking engagements were canceled overnight, but my finances never slowed down.

Everything changed when I discovered and implemented the secret the elite have used for decades. It is how they prospered even during the Great Depression and some of the worst recessions in history. Their strategy works.

| ‖‖‖‖‖‖‖‖‖‖‖‖‖ **FINANCIAL FAST TRACK FACT** ‖‖‖‖‖‖‖‖‖‖‖‖‖ |

THE FIRST STEP IN STOMPING OUT YOUR CREDIT CARD DEBT IS TO IDENTIFY THE REAL PROBLEM.

What Seems to Be the Trouble?

This chapter describes the road map my wife and I used to crush $180,000 of bad debt and build generational wealth without developing a scarcity or minimalist mindset. It will help you build a financial fortress that economic crises cannot penetrate. And because we road tested it, I know that it works.

When we were drowning in consumer debt, media personalities said our debt was the problem. Their solution was simple: climb out. A televangelist at the time even created the Debt Free Army, which I joined. I declared war on debt and focused on eliminating it.

The televangelist was well-intentioned. Bad debt is ugly. But guess what happened? I accumulated more debt. You know the drill: whatever you focus on grows. My mind was on contraction rather than expansion. I tried shrinking my lifestyle, hoping that my stack of bills would shrink too. I was obsessed with the problem instead of the solution. So, the problem metastasized.

I remember speaking at a church where thousands worshiped. The pastor and I were discussing my material when he said, "We have a training program that thousands of people go through each year to get free of debt."

I asked, "How many of them have succeeded?"

He admitted, "We've had one or two families."

Thousands of people have gone through the training, yet only one or two families conquered their debt? How can that be? This was no fly-by-night program. To this day, it is a household name. How can it fail so many people?

The problem is not the intent but the principle at work. If contraction is your goal, you cannot help but attract more of it. When getting out of debt was my number one goal, I could barely think of anything else. All my energy flowed toward cutting back, scrimping, and living below my means. Yet all I got was more poverty and lack—exactly what most poor and middle-class people experience when they try to fix their debt.

As your coach, I want you to shift toward abundance thinking. It simply means that your mind is aimed at ever-increasing wealth. When you dial into abundance thinking, your energy flows in that direction. Dwell on increase, and increase is what you get.

I remember how small thinking cornered me. Instead of thinking higher, I shrank my vision and tried to squeeze myself into it. In his classic book, *Think and Grow Rich*,[73] Napoleon Hill echoes the idea of Proverbs 23:7: "As [a man] thinketh in his heart, so is he" (KJV). Essentially, you are what you eat. If you feed on poverty thinking, you will become impoverished. You can follow the advice of yesterday's financial gurus. However, I warn you: you're punching your ticket for the slow boat to China.

Debt is not your real problem. It certainly wasn't for Bonnie and me, regardless of how much debt we had. Our lives changed when we realized that income was the root of our trouble. We needed more money coming in, money that would eliminate our debt and help us build massive wealth.

Three Economic Mindsets

There are real differences in how three economic classes approach tough times. As you read this section, identify any mindsets that you have wrongly accepted as truth. Becoming consciously aware of them is the beginning of breaking free.

For the poor, stress is always present. When lack increases their stress, they conclude that nothing is working for them. So, they search for outside solutions—someone or something "stronger" that can save them. Meanwhile, the rich and powerful respond by promising handouts, "easy" fixes, and a "steady" but meager income. They court the poor and reinforce their sense of helplessness. The stressed-out masses end up sacrificing their power to prosper by putting their trust and themselves in the government's hands.

The middle class reaches a similar conclusion: they find that despite their hard work, their finances don't improve. Selling their time for "security" has only plunged them deeper in debt. So, to survive, they clip coupons, tighten their purse strings, and downsize their lives.

The rich approach money completely differently. Instead of shrinking their lives to fit into financial limitations, they look for ways to increase income. They leverage the tough times by solving new problems! Therefore, they thrive when everybody else is struggling.

---

73 Napoleon Hill, *Think and Grow Rich* (Robbinsdale, MN: Fawcett Crest, 1983).

The rich minimize the impact of their debt by enlarging their resource pool. They add additional income streams that absorb the impact of downturns and other negative events. The mindset of the rich is not constrictive. It's expansive.

```
||||||||||||||||||||||||| FINANCIAL FAST TRACK FACT |||||||||||||||||||||||||

INCOME, INCOME, INCOME—THE
SOLUTION TO ALL YOUR PROBLEMS.
```

Repeat after me: "Income cures all." I know saying that rattles some religious demons, but it's true, and they know it. They understand that money is connected to every area of life. The diagram below shows just a few of the money connections that continually affect us.

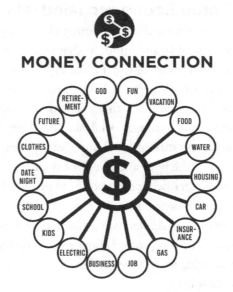

MONEY CONNECTION

Which of these areas causes you stress and worry? What if you could fix them? The question is important because fixing the money thing fixes everything. You know by experience that when your money is wrong, life feels wrong. When your money is right, the weight lifts from your shoulders, and your confidence returns.

So, yes, income cures all, and I'll prove it. Imagine that I promised to write you a $10,000 check every month. Would that reduce your financial stress?

I'm guessing you'd say, "Well, yeah!"

Did I shrink your debt? No. I brought you an income solution. Flow another stream of income from Dr. Keith Johnson into your life, and your $3,000 monthly credit card payment no longer seems like a problem.

That's why I say, "Income cures all."

> *Invest what you have in several different businesses because*
> *you don't know what disasters might happen.*
> —ECCLESIASTES 11:2 (NCV)

My One-Income-Stream Debacle

History's first trillionaire was probably King Solomon. He had multiple income sources, including his salary as monarch, shipping revenues from trade routes he organized and controlled, and an international consulting empire (more on this in chapter 13).

King Solomon was rich because he understood that no matter how much faith you have, how good a person you are, how much you give to your church, or how hard you work, unforeseen events can impact your financial streams.

The question is how you will fortify those streams to keep negative events from stealing, killing, and destroying your financial health. I learned this lesson a little late. Back in 2001, my only income stream was my speaking business. When the September 11 attacks came, my speaking gigs went up in smoke. For the next six months, my income was $0.00.

That's when I racked up $180K in bad debt. Bonnie and I lived off our credit cards. When one card's payment came due, we used another card to pay it. We kited payments to be sure we could open one more card. By the time we maxed out thirty-nine credit cards, the offers for more cards stopped coming.

I still remember a certified letter from American Express. They wanted me to sign a document promising that I would not go bankrupt. They saw that our house of cards was about to come down. We knew we were sunk and couldn't lie to ourselves or anyone else any longer.

What we needed was a "Lake of Wealth" that would change everything.

Feed Your Lake of Wealth

Solomon had the multiple streams of income idea exactly right. He understood that one was not enough. Take a good look at the diagram below. Notice the two sides of the mountain. One has a pond or desert. One has a nice big lake.

The left side of the mountain represents the finances of most poor and middle-class people. No matter how good they are or how much they earn, they still have just one income stream, typically a job. When the income flows, it collects in a pond. It's not a large body of water, and the stream that feeds it is vulnerable.

If something impacts that stream—an unfortunate workplace situation, a job-killing error, downsizing, an acquisition or merger, an injury, a company closure, or a pandemic—that solitary stream dries up, and the pond becomes a desert.

Can you see why having a job as your single stream of income is the riskiest path to wealth? Even a temporary interruption can be disastrous. And the longer it lasts, the larger your debt load becomes.

> ‖‖‖‖‖‖‖‖‖‖‖‖‖‖‖‖‖‖‖ **FINANCIAL FAST TRACK FACT** ‖‖‖‖‖‖‖‖‖‖‖‖‖‖‖‖‖‖‖
>
> ## MOST PEOPLE HAVE MULTIPLE STREAMS OF BILLS INSTEAD OF MULTIPLE STREAMS OF INCOME.

Now look at the right side of the mountain, where wealthy people live. While 95 percent of the poor and middle class struggle from paycheck to paycheck, the top 5 percent see an entirely different picture. The key on their side of the mountain is having multiple income streams flowing into a nice, big, deep Lake of Wealth.

The right side of the mountain is not entirely secure. Catastrophes can affect the whole mountain. However, those who maintain multiple streams of income have numerous sources of cash. When one income stream slows down, certain other streams can continue to produce.

Before I began to earnestly build my Lake of Wealth, my speaking business was my only cash producer. When that crashed, my pond became my desert. Then I awakened to the wisdom of the wealthy and committed to creating more income streams. Adding a second stream changed our lives. But we didn't stop there, and neither should you. Commit to giving God multiple ways to flow your resources.

One word of caution about adding income streams: I don't endorse harebrained schemes. You don't build your Lake of Wealth by jumping into a whole new profession or enlisting in an unproven, unvetted multilevel marketing program. You might be tempted do something random, but it will probably do you more harm than good.

People often choose real estate when adding an income stream. We have all seen reality shows about flipping houses or purchasing apartment buildings. I'm not saying you can't make money in real estate. You can. But unless you first become an expert, rookie decisions will empty your pockets.

Be wise. Start diversifying by strengthening your first flow. Begin to grow or add skills in your current profession. Then find a supplemental service or product. Instead of operating outside your genius, maximize it.

⊔⊔⊔⊔⊔⊔⊔⊔⊔⊔⊔ **FINANCIAL FAST TRACK FACT** ⊔⊔⊔⊔⊔⊔⊔⊔⊔⊔⊔

DON'T DEVELOP ANOTHER INCOME STREAM UNTIL YOU HAVE THE KNOWLEDGE AND WISDOM TO SUSTAIN IT.

I strengthened the flow of my speaking business by landing more speaking opportunities. Then I started offering coaching and consulting services. Leveraging my existing platform was logical. To make it work, I committed to learning, studying, and increasing my knowledge and skills as a coach.

Once my second stream produced financial increase, I sought a third income stream. It seemed that as a speaker and coach, I could also offer a book. So, I wrote through the nights until I became an author.

That's what I mean by making money in my underwear. When I climb into bed at night, my phone stands watch as the money comes in. It says, "Ding. Ding. Ding!" Every sound is a sale. It might be a book I wrote years ago or a course from a seminar I taught. I did the work once, but the stream keeps filling my lake, even while I'm sleeping.

Forgive my skepticism, but another harebrained scheme makes me chuckle. It's the "magic of compound interest." Interest is fine, but how can you build wealth from a savings account that earns less than one half of 1 percent interest? Are you serious?

How about compounding your streams of income instead? Use the raw power of multiplication to transform your financial position. Remember the debt problem you had when your job stream was your sole support? With multiple income streams flowing, your Lake of Wealth will swallow up that debt and eliminate it!

I hate to say, "I told you so," but you can see that debt is not the problem. Not having a big Lake of Wealth is. So, I keep adding income streams. More and more products, such as informational and training materials (like this book) became the foundation of Destiny College. Then those successful streams helped create my real estate stream. By acting intentionally, I have developed eight income streams:

1) Speaking
2) Coaching
3) Destiny College

4) 83K Academy

5) Wealth Tribe

6) Investments

7) Real Estate

8) Products

If you think you can't add streams of income to protect you from unwelcome events, you are wrong. You can do it, and you should. If the COVID-19 pandemic has proved anything, it's the wisdom of diversified sources of income.

Let that wisdom change your life.

When Life Punches You in the Face

My first financial crisis began with the September 11 terrorist attacks. The second followed a heart attack, but, by then, I had other income streams and was far less vulnerable.

When my doctors said, "You can't travel or speak before audiences for the next six to eight months," that income stream was cut off. But I could still coach clients virtually. And I could sell products, enroll students into Destiny College, and earn money from real estate.

What excites me is knowing that the season after my heart attack was one of the most prosperous of my entire life. Disruptions are inevitable. But when multiple income streams kick in, good stuff happens anyway. Even when my coaching business dipped, or the Florida real estate market dropped, something else took off. At one point, my speaking business saw a huge upswing. Considering the many fluctuations I have experienced, I'm thankful for what multiple income streams can do!

My point is that you don't have to depend on one income source. Build streams inside of your existing expertise. In my case, I was familiar with coaching, teaching, course creation, and writing. All of it was wrapped inside my genius which is centered on the information industry. Only later did I invest in other arenas, such as real estate.

That is the model to follow. Begin with flows that are related to your current career or business. Make the most of the time, effort, energy, and finances you have already invested. Leverage them! If you've had only one job or career, pinpoint your expertise. You know things that most other people don't know. That makes you an expert.

Of course, there are levels of expertise. If you have been playing guitar for a week and know two chords, you're an expert to someone who first picked up the instrument this morning. To that person, what you know has value. Some schools of thought say that if you've read three books on a subject, you are an expert. Still others preach that you need ten thousand hours under your belt to qualify.

The fact is that we live in a time when everyone can declare themselves experts, and many people do. If you are dedicated to your craft, and people can benefit from your knowledge, your expertise has value.

Pick Two Streams

No matter where you are in your journey, I invite you to consider two income-producing enterprises that are the easiest and the first ones I recommend:

1) Become a coach.

2) Become an author.

Remember that you are living in the Information Age. Package the right information for the right market, and you can sell it for a premium. But why coaching? Coaching requires a minimum start up. In fact, you could begin with a ninety-day mentoring experience, a computer, and a cell phone. If you have expertise, you are qualified to help others grow in your profession. You could make hundreds or thousands of dollars for a few hours of your time each month. And here's the best part: you can do that every month.

With your coaching underway, start writing, immediately. A book is the perfect fuel for your coaching stream. See it as a paid-for business card. When someone purchases your $20 book, they might also seek a more hands-on relationship through your coaching. Even those who haven't read your book will see you as an expert *because* you are an author. Readers and others can then seek your advice.

Every quarter, through my 83K Academy, I mentor a small group of aspiring speakers, coaches, and authors on building a million-dollar expert empire (see chapter 14). The academy is one of my income streams. I figured out that if billionaires and multimillionaires have multiple streams of income, and companies like Apple have even more (think iPhones, iPads, Macs, Apple watches, iTunes, Apple TV, the App store, iCloud, and more), I should offer a diverse line of products and services too.

Swimming the Streams Around You

You don't need a PhD to know where your strengths and expertise are. Have you had great success as a pastor who counsels struggling couples? Are you a worship leader who can teach piano? Maybe you sell advertising and can teach business owners how to craft compelling ads.

You might not see your job knowledge as having that type of potential. Let's say you're a warehouse worker. Do you have any ideas about how to pick orders faster? Is there a way to stock shelves so that the accuracy and speed of order picking are enhanced? Maybe you have learned how to pack goods in ways that reduce damages. That knowledge can reduce a company's damage claims and improve its bottom line.

Whatever your expertise, you can systematize your ideas in a book and publish it through Amazon. Now imagine that your book's final chapter includes your contact information for those who want to get started in your coaching system. You have just created a lead-generating tool that sells your coaching services. One of your income streams is feeding another!

It's been said that the average millionaire has three to seven (or more) streams of income. So, what is stopping you as a stay-at-home mom or warehouse worker or pastor or landscaper from earning six or seven figures a year?

Really, only one or two things could stop you. One is possibility blindness and the other is the sedentary act of making your cable provider rich. You are worth more than that. Go ahead and make yourself rich. You can have more. You can help more. And you have more to give.

Are you ready? The world is, and with other people's money, you can reach them.

· · · · · · · · · ·

FINANCIAL FAST TRACK COACHING

1) How (and in how many ways) can you strengthen your current stream of income?

2) Think about this chapter and ask yourself, *What income stream can I add today?* List your ideas below. Yes! Amaze yourself by coming up with seven.

1. _____

2. _____

3. _____

4. _____

5. _____

6. _____

7. _____

3) What class or course should you take to gain more knowledge, understanding, and wisdom about how to build this new stream?

4) Who could serve as your mentor? How will you connect with that person?

5) Take time for some imagineAction! What three things will you do in the next ninety days to start building a new income stream?

1. _____

2. _____

3. _____

FINANCIAL
FAST TRACK

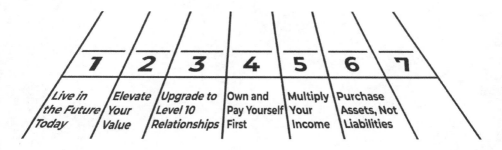

1	2	3	4	5	6	7
Live in the Future Today	Elevate Your Value	Upgrade to Level 10 Relationships	Own and Pay Yourself First	Multiply Your Income	Purchase Assets, Not Liabilities	

11

LEVERAGE OPR TO INCREASE ASSETS: BUILD WEALTH AND ELIMINATE LIABILITIES

What do Chick-fil-A, Apple, Google, Nike, Disney, Facebook, Chipotle, Dyson, Virgin Atlantic Airways, and the widow in 2 Kings chapter 4 have in common? They all used *other people's resources* (OPR) to start, grow, and scale their cash-flowing businesses, build their brands, and accumulate wealth.

When the widow in 2 Kings 4 lost her husband, her income instantly dried up. They were in debt before he died. But without him, she saw no hope of digging out. The situation was so bad that their creditors were about to take her sons as slaves. She had already lost her husband, her income, and whatever financial confidence she had left. Now she was going to lose her boys too.

What happened next is amazing!

The wife of a man from the company of the prophets cried out to Elisha, "Your servant my husband is dead, and you know that he revered the Lord. But now his creditor is coming to take my two boys as his slaves."

Elisha replied to her, "How can I help you? Tell me, what do you have in your house?"

"Your servant has nothing there at all," she said, "except a small jar of olive oil."

Elisha said, "Go around and ask all your neighbors for empty jars. Don't ask for just a few. Then go inside and shut the door behind you and your sons. Pour oil into all the jars, and as each is filled, put it to one side."

She left him and shut the door behind her and her sons. They brought the jars to her and she kept pouring. When all the jars were full, she said to her son, "Bring me another one."

But he replied, "There is not a jar left." Then the oil stopped flowing.

She went and told the man of God, and he said, "Go, sell the oil and pay your debts. You and your sons can live on what is left." —2 Kings 4:1–7 (NIV)

Amid her chaos, God sent the widow a financial deliverer. The prophet Elisha listened to her story and provided the solution that produced unexpected income and eliminated her debt. When all seemed lost, the answer gave her and her sons lasting financial stability.

The solution Elisha crafted was simple:

1) Go borrow.
2) Start an oil-selling business.
3) Pay off your debt.

Breathe that in for a moment. Then let's bust up some myths.

Down with Debt Mythology

I have heard television and radio personalities swear that Scripture never tells us to borrow. Well, this passage rebuts that claim. The prophet outright told the widow to borrow vessels. That loan empowered her to wipe out her debt and save her sons.

Her turnaround was fantastic, and so was mine. Borrowing helped me to climb out of $180,000 worth of bad debt. But why stop with the widow and me? What about Jesus? Did He borrow?

Yes, He used OPR. Here are some examples that we know about:[74]

> » He borrowed a fishing boat from Peter (Luke 5).
> » He borrowed a donkey that had never been ridden (Luke 19).
> » He borrowed a sack lunch from a young boy (John 6).
> » He borrowed a room from a man with a pitcher of water (Mark 14).
> » He borrowed a rich man's tomb for His burial (John 19).

Jesus said, "Give to the one who asks you, and do not turn away from the one who wants to borrow from you" (Matthew 5:42, NIV). If it is wrong in God's eyes

---

74 Others have written about this from a variety of angles. Tim Price's blog post is a great read: Tim Price, "Jesus Borrowed," *Tim Price Blog*, 14 Nov. 2019, https://www.timpriceblog.com/jesus-borrowed/.

to borrow, then it must be wrong to lend to others. If one were right and the other wrong, God would be contradicting Himself, which He would never do.

|||||||||||||||||||||||| FINANCIAL FAST TRACK FACT |||||||||||||||||||||||||

IF IT'S WRONG TO LEND, THEN IT MUST BE WRONG TO BORROW. IF IT'S RIGHT TO LEND, THEN IT MUST BE RIGHT TO BORROW. DO BOTH WISELY.

Many pastors, theologians, and wannabe Bible experts who have no track record as successful businesspeople use a few popular scriptures to condemn borrowers. Predictably, they refer to Romans 13:8, which says, "Owe no man any thing" (KJV). I would contend that if you pay your bills on time, you are honoring your commitment and technically don't owe anyone.

You have probably heard that "the borrower is servant to the lender" (Proverbs 22:7). If you are borrowing to cover your financial liabilities, you are the lender's servant. But if you are borrowing to create cash-flowing assets, the lender becomes your servant.

Another go-to verse says, "You shall lend to many nations, but you shall not borrow" (Deuteronomy 28:12). This scripture suggests the divine possibilities that arise when nations or people borrow from us. Realistically, however, we don't start our financial journeys this way. We start on the bottom needing help from other people's resources.

> *Borrowing is the ladder of grace to the underprivileged and the*
> *poor to help them climb out of the sewers of poverty.75*
> —DR. KEITH JOHNSON

White, upper-middle-class money teachers claim it is wrong to borrow. Yet they take on mortgages to purchase homes in swanky suburban neighborhoods. Meanwhile, my black and brown brothers and sisters in the inner city are fighting for equal lending practices. They want to purchase their share of the American dream, and OPR is the answer.

---

75 From a video I once did about the "Wealthy Church."

My good friend, Rabbi Daniel Lapin, the best-selling author of *Thou Shall Prosper*, said something that puts our scriptural concerns in perspective:

> *Too many people read a proverb or a cute cultural saying in the Bible and turn it into a must do always principle to live by under all circumstances. But a proverb or witty and rhyming phrases have to be used with wisdom according to the current situation. A proverb that is wise in one situation or season isn't necessarily wise in another.*[76]

Knowing history can demystify the issue of borrowing. The modern banking system began with Jewish people who wanted to solve a big problem for God's children. They began by helping poor and struggling entrepreneurs get capital to start or scale their small businesses. Am I suggesting that lenders never overstep their bounds? No. I am saying that lenders offer a service that we can use wisely.

You might already know that before 1971, our money got its value from gold. Under President Nixon, however, we moved from the gold standard to a system in which money derives its value from debt. Please get this! The entire system is backed by debt. Borrowing money is what makes the system work.

Like it or not, you have to learn how to play the financial game. Until you do, you will either lose outright or ride that slow, expensive boat to China. If you want to prosper, you need to understand the rules and then leverage them to your advantage.

You also need to examine your thinking. How you interpret the word *debt* depends entirely on your belief system. So, what thoughts come to your mind when I say that word? If you grew up in the poor or middle class, you were probably conditioned to see debt as a millstone around your neck. If you are a Christian, you likely see debt as a sin. But if you are wealthy, you see it very differently.

Why? Because the rich see debt as a resource. They use other people's money as an opportunity—not to dig themselves a permanent hole but to become successful investors who can build their dreams faster.

Borrowing is the wealthy class's way of purchasing cash-flow assets and creating financial freedom. Think *borrow* not *debt*.

The Financial Mountain

All of us are somewhere on our journey up a financial mountain. Everyone wants to reach the top, but almost no one starts there. You have to *climb* the mountain. That means choosing from multiple paths to the top. As you know, I prefer quick routes because we live in a fast world where slow movers tend to get marooned at the bottom.

---

76 Rabbi Lapin shared this at the COVID 19 Emergency Wealth Summit, which I hosted in March of 2020.

The Financial Progress Mountain below maps out four basic levels on your upward path. The idea is to reach the top, where the investor-entrepreneurs live. Below them are business owners, and below them are employees. At the very bottom are the students. That is where most of us begin. The goal is not to make permanent camp there but to develop skills and move on.

To fully grasp this chapter, you must acknowledge that there is a financial mountain to climb. You probably started out as a student and then became an employee. Most of us stop our climb there. But if you continue upward, you can own your own business. Then your goal is to hire employees, serve them, and expand your earning potential.

Owning a business is a great step, but your ultimate goal is to become an investor-entrepreneur. Then you can use your cash along with other people's resources to purchase cash-flow assets. In other words, you make more money by raising capital. OPR enables you to build assets such as businesses, franchises, real estate, licenses, royalties, and online courses. That last item is not the lowest item, by the way. Online courses and other forms of intellectual property are essential to the Financial Fast Track.

Investors reach the mountaintop largely by using OPR to make more money. Their motto is, "Not with my money, you don't." The true investor-entrepreneur gets the importance and value of selling a dream to other investors who then join in funding their projects.

Raising capital and attaining assets also positions you to eliminate your liabilities. It's a matter of leverage, and it's all part of how Financial Fast Track #6 works. You can use your own resources along with OPR to purchase assets that produce income. Applying *leverage* means finding ways to achieve more with less effort. When you use more of other people's money and less of your own, that's leverage. The same is true of leveraging time. Hiring employees enables you to use less of your time while becoming more productive.

Remember that working harder is not synonymous with making more money. First, you want to work smarter through leverage. Then working harder will pay off, and you will scale your financial mountain.

Leveraging OPR Like a Billionaire Would

If I could permanently erase the word *debt* from your mind, I would. But I can't, so let's reprogram your thinking instead. Whenever you hear the word *debt*, I want you to think, "Other people's resources." Debt is OPR. The wealthiest people in your area are using it because they recognize the advantage of other people's money in building their own financial wealth.

Want to see if I'm right? Conduct your own case study. Hop in your car and cruise down Main Street. Notice the businesses lined up like sardine cans—the franchise coffee shops, apartment complexes, gas stations, restaurant chains, and big-box stores. Ninety-nine percent of them are leveraging OPR from government grants, banks, and private investors. Many of them are owned by multimillionaire investors who have learned to use OPR to launch, grow, and scale their businesses and financial status.

Did you know that banks are leveraged borrowers? They don't use their profits to loan money to others. They leverage ridiculously low interest rates through Fannie Mae and Freddie Mac. Then they make money on what they borrowed from the government. Borrowing OPR at 1 percent and selling it to consumers like you and me at 3 percent plus interest—that's a good bit of leveraging.

FINANCIAL FAST TRACK FACT

TO BECOME A LENDER, YOU MUST THINK THE WAY INVESTORS AND BANKERS THINK.

Now that your understanding of OPR is clearer, let's define some terms that will increase your financial intelligence and financial confidence.

Asset: This is a business or investment that consistently provides cash flow to its owner or holder. Examples include, businesses, books, courses, or programs sold online; multi-unit properties; consultancies, etc. Notice my emphasis on intellectual properties (books, courses, etc.). They are game changers because everyone has some knowledge or expertise that people need and will pay to acquire.

Borrow: To borrow is to use something that belongs to someone else and then return it. Borrowing also refers to using someone else's money with the agreement to pay it back over an agreed span of time.

Debt: Debt is what you owe to an individual, bank, or organization from which you borrowed. If you promised to pay by a certain date and failed to fulfill that obligation on time, you are indebted. For example: you agreed to pay the bank $500 on the first day of every month for your car note. Pay on that date and you are not in debt. Pay on the next day, and you are. You have also broken your word, which is unethical.

Liability: When you spend money that produces no return either now or in the future, it is a liability. For example, purchases that depreciate over time are liabilities. They include your cars, credit card payments, Disney vacations, clothing, and sushi dates.

OPR: Other people's resources can be borrowed for free or for an agreed-upon cost (interest) to create or purchase an asset. Examples include cash and personal loans, credit cards, mortgages, and equipment.

The terminology is simple enough. So is the Financial Fast Track philosophy, which is to become trustworthy by being ethical and paying your bills on time. Then you can leverage OPR to purchase income-producing assets, quickly build financial abundance, and significantly reduce or eliminate your liabilities.

Using OPR demonstrates your financial confidence to generate money and pay people back in the future. Why? Because you believe in your ability to earn, multiply, and distribute money wisely. It reflects not a poverty mindset, but a wealth mindset.

Mindsets define us. People apply to my 83K Academy because they want to build their expert empires and intellectual assets. Yet they often say, "I don't have any money to build my business."

I understand what they mean. They don't have boxes of extra cash lying around. But most of them have opportunity staring them in the face. They forget to tap their imaginations for a way forward because a narrow point of view stops them cold. They see their limitations very clearly—much more clearly than they see their opportunity.

If you have a similar "vision problem," remind yourself that OPR is your way forward. You can get the resources you need to build your dream. Let's look at the two types of resources you can use to build more assets:

1) **Free OPR:** Resources and money you receive at no cost, for the building or purchasing of an asset

2) **Cost OPR:** Resources or money you accept at an agreed-to cost (fees and/ or interest), for the building or purchasing of an asset

Now, let's get creative and explore our two options, beginning with free OPR. You can see that free OPR comes from a variety of places.

FREE OPR FROM:	
Immediate family members	State incentives
Other relatives	Interested strangers
Friends	A struggling business or retiring owner who might turn over an existing business
Grants	

If your free options fail, seek OPR that comes with a cost of your time or money, as in the examples below.

INTEREST-BEARING LOANS FROM:
Financial institutions
Family members
Friends
The Small Business Administration (SBA)
The seller of a business you take over
A company or organization
BARTERING **(Trading your time for needed resources)**

Learn from Reliable Sources

Are you still saying, "I just want to be debt free"? I know you were taught that having zero debt is the ultimate symbol of a successful, peaceful, and happy life, but it's not. In fact, it is often a sign of self-imposed constraints leading to failed, tormented, and miserable outcomes.

I'm not advocating bad debt. Bad debt is *bad.* But using OPR to create cash-flow assets is not bad debt. If having no debt ensured your success, I suppose those without roofs over their heads should feel successful. However, one look in their pained faces can tell you that's just not the case.

############################ **FINANCIAL FAST TRACK FACT** ############################

THE NEW "GOLD RUSH" IS THE ABILITY TO ACCESS LARGE AMOUNTS OF OPR FOR THE PURCHASE OF ASSETS.

Having the right information is critical to your thought process and your wealth. Therefore, I'm choosy about teachers. The folks in the peanut gallery can't help me grow. I need to learn from people who have done what I feel called to do. So, when a billionaire friend invited me to be his guest at the success conference he was hosting, I jumped at the chance.

For a solid day, I sat in on forty-five-minute interviews with billionaires. Yes! Every forty-five minutes, another billionaire took the stage. Every single one emphasized the importance of using OPR to purchase assets and build their dreams.

Please hear me: you can learn from a bum, a billionaire, or someone in between. I'm not looking to model my financial intelligence after a millionaire-next-door type of philosophy. In fact, at some point I stopped wanting to learn from millionaires at all. I need to study the financial strategies of Level 9 billionaires. Remember: millionaires are the new middle class. I need to learn from billionaires and beyond.

To reach your next level, you must reset your mind for the right attack plan. That means listening to those who have done what you have in mind. Listen to what they have learned from their progress on the mountain and leverage it.

Debt Free Is Not Your Destination

Being debt free is not all it's cracked up to be. It is not a cure-all but a baseline measure, a financial ground zero. Many debt-free people are impoverished and unable to care for themselves or help others. You can be debt free and still be unable to invest in the storehouse.

That is why I'm so adamant about helping people pursue multiple streams of income! You can shrink yourself down and blend into the middle-class, khaki-pants-and-button-down-shirt crowd. You can become the inconspicuous millionaire next door and live a quiet, unassuming life. But many such millionaires have zero influence and are making little or no impact in the world. Some are glorified cheapskates who refuse to help others because they became millionaires through scarcity thinking. They have not learned the principles that can out-earn their fears.

Think in terms of the long game: your goal is to build a war chest of resources and leave a financial legacy to your grandchildren. That's how Jews think. Your Financial Fast Track goal isn't to be debt free. It is to be free of bad credit card debt and have millions of dollars invested in cash-flowing assets so you can leave behind generational wealth.

FINANCIAL FAST TRACK FACT

DEBT FREE IS GROUND ZERO. THE FINANCIAL FAST TRACK DOES NOT MEMORIALIZE GROUND ZERO. IT BUILDS, MULTIPLIES, AND DISTRIBUTES MONEY FOR THE BENEFIT OF MANY.

Remember that your income problem makes your debt loom large. So, getting more income-producing assets is your priority, and eliminating debt by multiplying cash flow is your plan of attack. The formula is simple: **multiply assets + reduce liabilities = accelerated financial results**.

The idea is to first invest in and create assets that produce recurring income. Then take a percentage of your profits and reinvest it to quickly reduce your liabilities (the mistakes you made with credit cards and consumer spending). Liabilities drain your ability to store and invest in sound assets.

People often ask, "How should I reduce my liabilities and credit card expenses quickly?" I consider myself to be in business with God. He knows where the gold is, and He knows the perfect strategy to help you quickly eliminate your liabilities. What works for someone in a nine-to-five job differs from what a business owner needs.

There are many approaches to take. Over the years, I have seen all of them succeed for my coaching clients. To find the right one, each person had to consider many factors, including their giftings, geography, and financial intelligence. Once they found the strategy that met their needs, they simply had to *stick with it.*

〰〰〰〰〰〰〰〰〰〰 **FINANCIAL FAST TRACK FACT** 〰〰〰〰〰〰〰〰〰〰

FIND A BAD-DEBT ELIMINATOR
PLAN. THEN STICK WITH IT.

Where your liabilities are concerned, the most important thing you can do is to attack them *now*! Study your options and choose a fast strategy. The following are my top seven. Some of them are quicker than others. More than one might suit your needs.

FAST ATTACK

Strategy #1: Multiply Your Income

Ask yourself, *How can I double, triple, quadruple, or even multiply my income by a factor of ten this year?* Focus 70 percent of your time on increasing your first and strongest income streams. Then, spend 30 percent of your time building additional streams. Build your Lake of Wealth and let it swallow your debt, as we discussed in the previous chapter.

Strategy #2—Go Bankrupt

You probably have not heard this taught in church, but bankruptcy is a biblical concept related to the year of the jubilee (as laid out in Leviticus 25). Jubilee was instituted by God as a pattern for canceling all debt every fiftieth year. You could say it's a compassionate feature of capitalism, but it began as God's grace for borrowers.

Based on the biblical model, the United States encourages risk takers to borrow money and build businesses. From a government standpoint, these risk takers create jobs for others. If their efforts fail, bankruptcy allows them to start over. If the COVID-19 pandemic taught us anything, it taught us that business owners take significant risks to add value in their communities.

Sadly, few people risk starting businesses. They are so afraid of failing that they never allow themselves to succeed, even though the government has provided a safety net to catch them. During the 2016 presidential campaign, then candidate Donald Trump responded to his opponent's criticism of a business bankruptcy by saying, "What I've done is I've used, brilliantly, the laws of the country."[77] Sometimes the smartest thing you can do is to stop the bleeding and start over, especially if the law has made provision for you to recover.

"The average millionaire goes bankrupt 3.5 times,"[78] and some do so before achieving a financial breakthrough. Before 1971, bankruptcy could ruin your ability to borrow for seven years or more. Today, within twenty-four hours after your bankruptcy is official, credit card offers come in the mail. Why? Because lenders know you can afford them.

Do your homework. If bankruptcy is your next step, consult a bankruptcy lawyer to determine the best strategy for you.

Strategy #3: Kill the Bear and the Lion

Before David killed Goliath, he killed "tamer" creatures, such as bears and lions. Many people in debt attempt to pay down their "Goliaths" first. Then they get discouraged and quit because the task seems so daunting.

---

77 David Wright, "Trump Defends 'Brilliantly' Using Bankruptcy Laws," *CNN*, 22 June 2016, https://www.cnn.com/2016/06/22/politics/donald-trump-defends-bankruptcy-history/index.html.

78 Brenda P. Wenning, "You Can Be a Millionaire!" *Milford Daily News*, 1 Aug. 2021, https://www.milforddailynews.com/story/business/2021/08/01/you-can-millionaire/5414798001/.

To eliminate your debt, start with your smallest monthly payment. Once you slay that beast, add the monthly installment amount to the payment of your next lowest bill. Achieving these "small" victories will give you the confidence and momentum you need to take down bigger game. Keep repeating the process until you get to your "Goliath." Then apply all your former payment amounts to finish him off.

This is an exciting strategy my wife and I used to eliminate our bad credit card debt more than ten years ago. Every time we wiped out a balance, we played the Queen song, "Another One Bites the Dust"![79]

Strategy #4: Make Minimum Payments Only

This strategy is for those who want to own a business but need capital to start, grow, or scale it for a season. The idea is to pay the lowest possible payments on all your credit cards while using the rest of your money to invest in yourself or your business. Once the business begins to boom, start using Strategies #1 and #3 to increase your income, kill the bear and the lion, and crush your bad debt.

Strategy #5: Start or Buy a Business (or a Larger Company)

Starting and buying businesses are Financial Fast Track mantras. A particular strategy when dealing with debt is for smaller businesses to buy larger ones. This enables the smaller firm to eliminate its debt and fix its negative cash flow. Larger firms generally have greater cash flow, and that influx of revenue can make the smaller company's debt insignificant.

This strategy can also shorten the timeline to profitability. A new business can take between one and five years to show a profit. Therefore, starting from scratch can waste your most finite asset which is time. Buying an existing business that is profitable or nearly profitable puts you on a fast track and can spare you some of those first lean years.

FINANCIAL FAST TRACK FACT

BUYING AN ESTABLISHED BUSINESS IS FASTER, EASIER, AND SMARTER THAN STARTING ONE FROM SCRATCH.

---

79 John Richard Deacon, "Another One Bites the Dust," Sony/ATV Music Publishing, LLC.

Many viable businesses are owned by aging founders who want to transition into retirement. Often, they lack someone to whom they can entrust their businesses and employees. Therefore, the right buyer can strike a very good deal.

When you buy an established business, you inherit the firm's financial history. This can make it easier to find OPR for the purchase. Also, some owners will agree that you pay them directly. Your payments then serve as the seller's monthly retirement income.

By far, buying a business is smarter and quicker. You can learn how to find, fund, and fix struggling businesses for big profits at BuyABusinessFastTrack.com.

FINANCIAL FAST TRACK FACT

RESPECT THE POWER OF OPR AND USE IT TO BUILD WEALTH.

Strategy #6: Buy Dirt

You know where I stand on real estate. If you have established your business and your opportunity storehouse, real estate will multiply your wealth. Why am I so sure of that? It's because, despite real estate's ups and downs, there is only so much property on Planet Earth. You can get more money. You can create more income streams, but there is only so much dirt you can buy. When you are prepared to add some to your fast track, buy wisely (more on that soon).

Strategy #7: Create Intellectual Property

Another Financial Fast Track mantra involves the creation of intellectual property. We will dive into this asset later in the chapter. For now, keep in mind that it is the most accessible, the least costly, and the most flexible asset in your portfolio. Create intellectual property, and it will create multiples income streams that can flow for a lifetime.

Before we move on, let me settle any misunderstandings of OPR.

First, other people's money can make you wealthy. But if misused, it can make you very poor. I agree with Dave Ramsey on certain basic principles. Cutting up your credit cards is good advice for people who cannot practice self-control. If you are hell-bent on charging up liabilities, so you can look rich, cutting your cards could be your only choice. For most people, however, flat-out refusing to use OPR is a self-limiting response that won't work on the fast track.

Second, to build financial intelligence you need to be crystal clear about the two types of borrowing you can choose:

1) **Bad borrowing:** This is your credit card debt from fancy dinners, impulsive fashion purchases, hair- and nail-salon visits, and "man toys" like sports cars, boats, guns, and new tools. This type of debt is a liability.

2) **Good borrowing:** This is the money you borrow to increase your value through personal development and by purchasing assets like businesses and multi-unit properties.

To keep it simple, good borrowing for asset purchases can fill your pockets, but bad borrowing will clean them out. With that in mind, let's take a quick look at the best investment of all.

Invest in Yourself

During Q & A sessions, people often ask, "What is the best place to invest my money?"

I answer with a question: "How much money have you invested in yourself over the past year?"

What you invest in yourself has the highest return on investment (ROI). Your greatest asset is *you*! Investing in yourself is good debt. Where OPR is concerned, investing in your business is great, but it's your second most important move.

When you hear the word *investments*, do you think about the stocks of other companies? Most people do. But why would you invest in other people's companies instead of your own? Don't you believe in You Inc. more than a firm over which you have no control?

If you're going to bet on something, bet on yourself. You are the biggest factor in your success. Years ago, a quote from business philosopher Jim Rohn changed my life. He said, "Success is not something you pursue. . . . Success is something you attract and accumulate by the person you become."[80] In other words, investing in yourself is the best investment you can make.

The Law of Personal Growth is a law of success. I have hung my hat on it for more than twenty years, and it has transformed my life and finances. Why? Because my level of achievement or personal income will rarely exceed my passion for personal development.

---

80 Jim Rohn, *Facebook*, February 7, 2013, https://www.facebook.com/OfficialJimRohn/posts/success-is-not-something-you-pursue-what-you-pursue-will-elude-you-it-can-be-lik/10152523315295635/.

To *earn* more you must *learn* more. Personal development means believing in your self-worth and future potential. Therefore, you give yourself permission to invest time, effort, and money in preparing to become your "future you."

What better investment can you imagine?

Leveraging OPR to Accelerate Wealth

You know how I feel about financial gurus who lay guilt trips on homeowners who still owe money on their homes. Guilt isn't helpful because people who feel condemned never thrive mentally. So, let me encourage you with some sanity: If you own a $300,000 house but owe the bank $150,000, you are not in debt. You are in equity.

That's right! If you owe less on your house than it's worth, pat yourself on the back, and say, "Good job!"

Now, if you owe the bank $152,000 on a house that's only worth $150,000, you are in housing debt. That's why I teach people not to buy houses at market value. If the market drops, you can find yourself in debt overnight. When you are shopping for a house, don't look for a good deal. Look for a steal.

While we are talking about houses, let me tell you what Bonnie and I did when we owed $180,000 in consumer debt. We borrowed more money to pay it off, but not in the way you might think. For $350,000, we purchased a home that needed renovation. We lived in it for nine years and then sold it for a huge profit. We did what the prophet Elisha told the widow to do: we used the money we made on the house sale to pay off our remaining debt.

No traditional teaching on debt would have suggested what we did. But had we listened to traditional thinking, we would still be carrying our debt and living in a less-than-advantageous area. Instead, we turned our home into an asset. Then we sold it, wiped out our remaining debt, and bought another house.

We repeated the process, renovating a house that we lived in for six years and flipping it for another huge profit. You can legally own and flip a home every two years. Provided you make less than $500,000 on the deal, you'll pay no taxes on the gains. Talk about a fast track for your finances!

So, are you wondering how to turn your home into an asset? Here are seven simple steps to follow:

1) Find a house that needs fixing up and buy it for a steal.
2) Live in the house.
3) Fix it up with the intention to sell.
4) Divorce the house.

5) List the house on Zillow to save on agent commissions.

6) Sell the house for a profit.

7) Repeat. Take your profit, and find another steal.

‖‖‖‖‖‖‖‖‖‖‖‖‖‖‖‖‖‖‖‖‖‖ **FINANCIAL FAST TRACK FACT** ‖‖‖‖‖‖‖‖‖‖‖‖‖‖‖‖‖‖‖‖‖‖

STAY MARRIED TO YOUR SPOUSE, NOT YOUR HOUSE.

The housing market generally increases between 5 and 7 percent annually. If you have $20,000 for a down payment, a bank will loan you up to $200,000 for a house. That means you stand to earn between 5 and 7 percent—not on your $20,000 but on the full value of the home.

Now, let's bump up the ante. If you have $200,000 and buy a $1 million house, you are earning between 5 and 7 percent on a million dollars instead of your $200,000. Your $1 million house will gain more than $276,000, while your $200,000 house will only produce around $55,000 in five years.

A pastor friend wanted to build his church the "Bible way," which to him meant building it debt free. After ten years, he was $100,000 away from completion. His congregation supported the project but was weary from their extended season of sacrifice. I suggested getting a loan for the remaining $100,000.

The pastor stuck to his three scriptures and whatever "God told him to do." Then COVID-19 hit. Now, the $100,000 of building materials needed to finish the job will cost $300,000. Meanwhile, his church can't grow because the sanctuary is too small to accommodate more people.

Was that good stewardship of God's money? I would say emphatically, "No!"

Another pastor was trying to buy a 25-acre lot debt free. I told him he should consider borrowing the money to purchase it. He changed his strategy and used OPR. In five short years, the property became prime real estate worth more than ten times his purchase price. He saved his church millions of dollars and glorified God by having one of the best locations in town. The church went on to become a megachurch.

Was this good stewardship of God's money? Did the people feel like they made a great investment in the kingdom? Definitely!

Money loves speed. Speed is one reason for America's wealth. Another is the OPR advantage, which can speed up the wealth-building process. Baby Boomers have more wealth than any generation in history. I believe greater access to borrowed money made that possible. In their pursuit to "keep up with the Joneses," they leveraged OPR and purchased more expensive assets.

Stop on a roadside in some parts of Africa, and you will see people selling the masonry blocks people use to build their homes. A few yards down the road, you will see a man carrying some of those blocks. Because access to OPR is so limited in many African nations, it is nearly impossible to get a house loan. Therefore, people must build their homes little by little, buying a few blocks at a time until the work is complete. They don't have any housing debt, but it can take between five and twenty years 'til their homes are complete.

The Zero-Money-Down Cash Flow Asset

I have now shared multiple strategies for eliminating liabilities and purchasing cash-flow-producing assets through the power of OPR. I have also mentioned what I believe is the best of all assets. You might not have thought about it as an asset, but you have been exposed to it. In fact, you have probably forked over your hard-earned money for the assets that made other people wealthy.

Have you ever been glued to an infomercial about buying real estate with no money down? Have you listened to someone else's expertise about getting rich? Sure you have. So have I. But who really got rich from those ads? Right—the person who sold the information.

And *that* is exactly what I want to show you.

Depending on your current financial confidence, purchasing a "hard" asset might seem out of reach. We have discussed many, but if you don't have the capital to buy a profitable business or a real estate portfolio right now, don't be discouraged. There is another asset class that requires no money to invest. It is intellectual property.

In 2009, Disney purchased Marvel Entertainment.[81] Three years later, they bought Lucasfilm. Disney acquired these assets for $4 billion apiece. But what exactly did they buy? Disney was after their competitors' intellectual property, and they got it. The deals included massive profits from Marvel blockbusters and "the *Star Wars* empire."[82]

---

81 Jamie Burton, "How Much Did Disney Buy Marvel for and When?" *Newsweek*, 12 June 2021, https://www.newsweek.com/how-much-did-disney-buy-marvel-when-mcu-1599404.

82 Burton, "How Much Did Disney . . . ?"

Disney purchased the power of intellectual property (IP).

IP is a nonphysical asset of original works of the mind that retains value only when secured under the legal protections of copyrights, trademarks, patents, or trade secrets. Disney recognized the inherent value of the existing IP it purchased and gladly forked over $8 billion.

Here's what I want you to recognize: if you have created an artistic or literary work, invention, design, or company brand, you have already developed intellectual property. I am not suggesting that you must create a comic book character or become a sci-fi filmmaker. But I am encouraging you to treat your thoughts like income-producing assets.

They are the most lucrative assets on the planet.

Every book, course, and program in my company is an asset. Through my imagination, I create product that I can sell in my sleep. I have even licensed my work, which means that other people pay for the privilege of using my IP to make money for themselves.

To get started in IP, I recommend that you write a nonfiction book, specifically, a "how-to" book. Realize, however, that your book has little value until you have a customer who will buy it. You don't have a business until you can sell your book.

That means you need to multitask. While you are creating your IP, you must also create a business asset. In our digital world, your greatest business asset is an email list. With a simple one-page website and an email opt-in form, you can cultivate an audience that is willing to pay for your work.

No matter what your industry or interests are, you should consider creating intellectual property to accelerate your impact, influence, and income. And if you would like my help to get your brand-building book ready, visit 83KAcademy.com.

Are your wheels turning yet? Mine are!

When you begin to see opportunity, you will receive opportunity. There is no shortage of money in the world. Money is abundant, and there is more than enough to fund your business, build your church, achieve your dreams, and buy the assets that create positive cash flow.

OPR can help you take control of your life. You're not a baby. You're a mature adult. Babies cannot be trusted to manage and leverage OPR to their advantage. But you can handle it, and you can create wealth in the process.

So, do you have the financial confidence to take your next leap? The next chapter will help you!

. . . .

FINANCIAL FAST TRACK COACHING

Get ready! It's time to create your quick attack plan.

1) List seven creative ways you can use OPR to purchase an asset capable of generating cash flow:

1. _____

2. _____

3. _____

4. _____

5. _____

6. _____

7. _____

3) Of the seven debt- and liability-eliminating strategies discussed, which one seems best suited to your situation, and why?

4) Describe in detail your next asset-building or liability-eliminating strategic move.

FINANCIAL
FAST TRACK

1	2	3	4	5	6	7
Live in the Future Today	Elevate Your Value	Upgrade to Level 10 Relationships	Own and Pay Yourself First	Multiply Your Income	Purchase Assets, Not Liabilities	Mind Your Business

12

MIND YOUR BUSINESS:
BUY, START, GROW, SCALE, AND SELL

Someone once told me, "My passion is to make a difference. I want to change the world and leave it better than I found it, like when Bill Gates fought to defeat malaria and save two thousand African children from death every day."

I frequently run into people who want to "change the world" and "make a difference." However, Bill Gates didn't start out by spending all his time, energy, and money saving children from malaria. He focused first on building a multibillion-dollar business that would serve the entire world. Through that business, he amassed the resources and influence to make a lasting difference in other ways.

The first step to making a difference is to make a fortune. In this chapter, we will discuss exactly that. It involves financial confidence, which begins with the sense of being *in control* of your circumstances. Without that control, you will lack confidence in yourself and your financial future. This is the reason 65 percent of people lose sleep to financial worry.[83] They know deep down that their outcomes are out of their hands.

One of the first things God provided for humankind's success was dominion, which is the ability to rule, manage, dominate, and control almost anything in the earth, other than each other. As always, God requires our participation. We cannot

---

83 According to a "USA Snapshot" survey by *Creditcards.com*.

be passive; we need to make choices. Four basic choices determine how we plan to accumulate "difference making" money:

1) A job
2) Investments
3) Real estate
4) A business

If you desire a level of control where making money is concerned, which of these choices qualifies? Your job isn't in your control. You could be fired tomorrow. Your 401K or stock investments aren't in your control. The entire system can implode tomorrow. We learned from the 2008 crisis that real estate values can drop by 50 percent in a month's time and plateau for ten years.

But what about a business you own? Can you control that? Yes, you have more control over your business than over any other option. And when you get that control, you naturally become more confident.

There is also the matter of making money quickly. If you are dreaming, hoping, and praying to make a quick million from a job, you are operating at the same level of insanity as someone who puts their hope in a lottery ticket. It might pay off someday, but it probably won't be soon.

How about making fast money from interest on your portfolio? If you are in the minority who love saving via compound interest savings accounts, that's wonderful. But with today's chronically low interest rates, you are running a marathon, not a sprint. The days of getting rich through compound interest are over.

So, how about real estate? I think this a great option, and I strongly believe in it but only after you have accumulated enough money in your storehouse. That means it's not the quick-attack move you need to start out. It is a long game and a strategic process.

So, do you have to own your own business for the Fast Financial Track to work for you? Frankly, *yes*. It is the only way to create wealth fast, and it gives you a much higher chance of success. Owning a business is your most reliable vehicle as you enter the fast track.

Losing Our Entrepreneurial Roots

My wife and I love our vacations on Paradise Island. On the back side of the Atlantis is a marina where some of the world's largest yachts are docked. It's a world most people never experience, and many never dream of.

Who buys those yachts, and why is that kind of wealth so distant from the masses? I think it is largely because we are brainwashed to become employees instead of entrepreneurs. We spend twelve to sixteen or more years being educated, or more accurately, being indoctrinated to take the slowest route to financial abundance.

That was my experience. Through all my years at school, I was never told about the possibility of owning my own business. I certainly was not taught how to start, grow, or scale one on my own. As the son of a business owner, I always wondered why.

Most people chase money and jobs instead of opportunities.[84]
—GRANT CARDONE

The concept of becoming an employee is more recent than you might think. During the Agricultural Age, people were entrepreneurs. They operated family farms or had private practices as blacksmiths, butchers, bakers, and barbers. Few people were employees, which contributed to slavery as a system of enforced work. Maybe that's why employees are called the "workforce." A modern-day workforce is not comparable to the brutality of enslaving human beings. However, it is as close as our society comes to "owning" people.

During the Industrial Age, the demand for employees grew exponentially. That is when government took over the educational system, which programmed the employee mindset and discouraged entrepreneurism. This was a significant shift, and its impact is massive.

Teaching on entrepreneurship was nonexistent because the powers that be needed people to conform. The masses were not to think, create, imagine, or color outside the system's lines because the system was built to benefit the powerful. They needed a force that would follow orders and uphold the system's objectives.

Simply put, they don't need your imagination; they want your muscles.

Think about the ratio of employees to business owners. It tilts overwhelmingly toward workers because the school system mass produces them. This program is controlled by the spirit of Mammon, which dominates people's decisions through the power of fear.

We are trained to fear. You are taught that if you get bad grades, you will flip burgers at McDonald's for the rest of your life. Failing grades will keep you from graduating high school and going to college. That means not getting a "good job" with benefits. You know—the benefits that allow you to retire on a shoestring in about forty years.

---

84   Grant Cardone, "Most people chase money and jobs instead of opportunities," Twitter.

If the fear of failing at school didn't crush you, your post-graduation fears might. Now employers (who have power over your paycheck) use fear to control you. They tell you to conform or be fired! The threat carries weight because with your job loss comes the loss of your 401K, health insurance, pension, and benefits.

With all of that gone, you fall behind on your mortgage payments. Then you fear the bankers taking your house. Next, your credit score plummets, and you lack the credit to rent a decent apartment. It is one huge cycle of fear with each component feeding into the others.

Ironically, the spiritual community preaches about how money, greed, and the spirit of Mammon control the rich. They say almost nothing about how Mammon threatens the poor and middle class through a system of fear, threats, and worry.

By the way, pastors are not exempt from these pressures. The system requires them to be church employees. While the spiritual community sings about freedom, they are oblivious to the fear that enslaves them, which means they aren't free at all.

Jesus and the Entrepreneurs

It is interesting that Jesus didn't call the spiritually minded people of His day to be His disciples. Instead, He pursued successful businesspeople, including commissioned tax collectors, commercial fishermen, political consultants, and doctors who owned private practices. Did you ever wonder why?

It is interesting to me that in Luke chapter 5, Jesus performed a prosperity miracle that filled Peter's boat and a second boat with fish. Immediately after that, Peter, James, and John "forsook all and followed Him" (Luke 5:11). They seem to have been attracted by more than Jesus' power to forgive, heal, and deliver.

Investor-entrepreneurs were among Jesus' earliest disciples, but today's church is full of job seekers and savers. Is it possible that a lack of teaching on Jesus' powers of prosperity is the reason our congregations include few successful business owners? Is that why churches have so many poor, sick, and oppressed people in their pews?

|||||||||||||||||||||||||||||||| **FINANCIAL FAST TRACK FACT** ||||||||||||||||||||||||||||||||

EMPLOYMENT IS THE PAST. THE FUTURE IS ENTREPRENEURSHIP.

I need to note here that if you work a job, you violate the "own and pay yourself first" rule of the Financial Fast Track. Why? Because the government always gets paid first. Your employer must withhold your tax money and give you whatever is left over.

As a corporation owner, I pay the government once each quarter. That means I pay my tithe and myself before I pay Uncle Sam. If a global crisis happens, I can put the good uncle on hold until I get my situation in order.

My point is that the wealth-in-a-wheelchair system was not built on godly values. As an employee, you are trapped in a life that other people control. You have no choice but to wait for your old-age money to materialize. Fear is inevitable because you can't pull the strings where *your* money is concerned.

It's no wonder so many people are chronically ill and addicted to coping mechanisms such as overeating, junk food, smoking, drugs, alcohol, video games, social media, and mindless TV binges. They are trying to deal with the pain of their unfulfilled potential!

If you are an employee, you spend your working years building something for someone else to pass down to their grandchildren. You can't sell your job to your replacement. You cannot bequeath it to your heirs. And you cannot control what that job gives you. You can accept your employer's terms or move on. And at the end of your working years, you might end up living on hot dogs and Hamburger Helper.

It is just not right.

FINANCIAL FAST TRACK FACT

YOU CANNOT LEAVE YOUR JOB AS AN INHERITANCE TO YOUR CHILDREN.

More Trouble Ahead

It doesn't look good for employees going forward. Uncertainty, rising costs, decreasing employer loyalty, and pressures to conform spell out difficult days for the workforce. Boomers see the writing on the wall, but as seniors, they often feel stuck. Especially since the COVID-19 pandemic, Millennials are skeptical about the job market and more interested in entrepreneurship. They see "sustainability and for-the-good focus" as being "missing from established industries."[85]

Let's look at some of the challenges employees have faced and will face in coming years.

The Future Doom of the Job Market

The global job market will become increasingly competitive, and the number of decent-paying jobs is expected to decline. One glance backward and you will see that while inflation surged over the past twenty years, wages largely plateaued.

Many higher-paying jobs are now outsourced to people in developing countries. Even CEOs and other C-level positions are being replaced by fractional CEOs in an outsourced, pay-as-you-go plan for executive positions.

How can wages go up when someone in India or Africa is willing to work for pennies? And what about artificial intelligence (AI)? How far will AI drive down the demand for employees? This situation has plagued Detroit auto workers since the development of robotics. But it's coming to all industries. Safe and secure jobs as we once knew them are disappearing for good.

The Truth About Taxes

If you are a professional investor or a business owner, most of your income is considered passive and is therefore taxed at the lowest rates. If you are an employee, your income is earned, making it the highest taxed money across many brackets. When employees earn more, the system penalizes them with more taxes. That sounds like an incentive for government and the education system to pop out wage earners rather than entrepreneurs. Follow the money, and the system makes sense.

I hope it is becoming clear to you that a job isn't as safe as it looks. It certainly isn't the wisest or fastest track to real prosperity.

So, how do you collect your first million dollars? You do it by increasing your financial education and thinking like an entrepreneur. Once you commit to this path, you will break out of the rat race and take your position on the Financial Fast Track. You will discover that everything you have been told about getting a job and finding success is clouded in deception and half-truths.

If you will pursue it, there is a much better way to live.

---

85 Nathan Peart, "COVID-19 Has Turned More Millennials into Serial Entrepreneurs," *Forbes*, 12 Dec. 2021, https://www.forbes.com/sites/nathanpeart/2021/12/29/covid-19-has-turned-more-millennials-into-serial-entrepreneurs/?sh=3d57edb23e5f.

Five Millionaire Mountains

You've decided to become rich. Now you must decide which millionaire mountain you are going to climb. There are five of them, pictured below.

I heard Brian Tracy speak on these primary opportunities where fortunes are made.[86] Let's dig into them a little.

1) **Entrepreneurship:** Seventy-four percent of millionaires began by starting, growing, and scaling a business. Examples include Henry Ford, Sam Walton, and Jeff Bezos.

2) **Executives:** Ten percent of millionaires are well-paid executives of successful companies. These are the CEOs, CFOs, and COOs of large corporations. This can include a firm's early employees who waive salaries and accept stock options or profit sharing. Examples include Bob Iger, Jamie Dimon, and Tim Cook.

3) **Professionals:** Ten percent of millionaires are highly degreed professionals such as doctors, lawyers, and engineers. These professions require advanced degrees for entrance.

4) **Sales professionals:** Five percent of millionaires are the highly skilled sales professionals in the top 5 percent of their companies. In most cases, they are commissioned salespeople who are paid strictly on the value they provide.

86   Brian Tracy, "Wealth Building Made Simple," disc 3. Tracy quoted the statistics regarding these groups some time ago. Although they have changed little, no two surveys have identical findings.

5) **Phenomena:** Only 1 percent of millionaires are music icons, professional athletes, movie stars, and lottery winners. The media would lead you to believe that this category produces the majority of success stories. That just isn't the case.

It is important to identify your options. When I was living in my mother-in-law's house, I was ready for a financial change. But I also needed financial confidence. That meant knowing which mountain offered the greatest chance of success.

I desperately wanted to provide for my family and avoid the pain and humiliation of poverty. I weighed my options and thought, *I don't have ten years to climb the corporate ladder and become an executive. I'm not smart enough. Nor can I afford medical school. God didn't give me the ability to rap like Jay-Z or shred a guitar like Eddie Van Halen. Nobody knows my pretty face in Hollywood. And I'm not seven feet tall. On my best day, I can't dribble a basketball like the late, great Kobe Bryant did.*

That left two options. I could start a career in sales or start a business. I decided to go for the highest chance of becoming a millionaire. So, I began building a coaching business that ended up generating millions of dollars.

That is how I did it, and that is how I recommend that you do it. My financial confidence mounted once I discovered that buying or building a business was my best chance to succeed. But I also needed to check out the idea from a spiritual perspective. That is when I ran into this powerful verse:

> Aspire to lead a calm and peaceful life as you mind your own business and earn your living, just as we've taught you. By doing this you will live an honorable life, influencing others and commanding respect of even the unbelievers. Then you'll be in need of nothing and not dependent upon others.
> —1 Thessalonians 4:11–12 (TPT)

The light went on! This scripture (which was taught by a Jewish tent-business owner) showed that building a successful business was an honorable endeavor that would increase my influence and command respect, not only in the church but in the marketplace. It also boosted my assurance that a business could provide abundance, and I would "be in need of nothing."

Of course, nothing could be clearer than what another Jewish man, Jesus Christ, said: "Do business—until I come" (Luke 19:13, YLT).

In other words, "Mind your business!"

Your Imagination Is Your E-Rocket Fuel

Les Brown has talked over the years about a survey of inner city children that posed this question: "What do you want to be when you grow up?" Some children said they wanted to be professional athletes, superstar singers, rappers, and movie stars. The problem is that only a tiny percentage—maybe 1 percent of people—have the physique or natural talent to succeed in those industries.

I have spent most of my life speaking in inner city churches to empower parents and children to go for their dreams. Sadly, many of those children see the 1-percent option as their only escape from the perils of poverty.

We need to teach our youth that voices like Whitney Houston's come once in a lifetime. Seven-time Super Bowl champion Tom Brady lives in a universe of one. And Hollywood careers like those of Samuel L. Jackson, Denzel Washington, Will Smith, and Kevin Hart are few and far between.

We must teach our children that each of them has a brain and an imagination. Therefore, the nonphenomena financial mountains are far more achievable than they think. They just need to gain knowledge and develop their financial and business intelligence. Instead of making heroes of the "phenoms," let's show our youth some heroes who are leading on the business mountain. Everyone can be trained to do that, including you.

Building a successful business is not a gig for funding sprawling mansions, exotic cars, and private jets. It is a calling and, therefore, an obligation. You discovered in Financial Fast Track #2 that adding value is what matters. Business adds value. That makes it a spiritual endeavor. Yes! Business is a spiritual exercise and a moral obligation. You must be intentional about doing more for others. Until you are, you won't succeed in business.

Your mission as an entrepreneur is to solve at least one meaningful problem for many people. The wealthiest entrepreneurs have something everybody wants. They take it upon themselves to be of profound service to others, and they serve on a massive scale. They make a difference and a dollar by climbing the ladder from local to global impact.

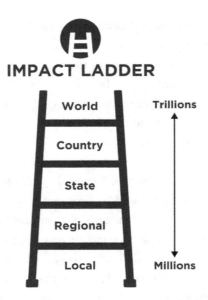

Help your local community, and you will make money. Help your region or state, and you will make more. Help your country, and you will make a lot of money. Help your continent, and you will become very wealthy. But if you are among the few who help the planet, you can become a billionaire or even a trillionaire.

Getting Down to Business

This succinct definition will help you buy, start, scale, and sell your business intelligently: a business is a commercial enterprise that creates a profit by solving problems and meeting the needs of the masses—and it does so without you.

If you desire to solve big problems for the masses (aka "achieve greatness"), a business of one is too small. Trust me; you can't do it alone. Technology allows you to declare yourself a business and offer services via the internet. I call this the rise of the solopreneur, a kind of business Lone Ranger who freelances or receives outsourced projects from other companies.

That is not a business. You might be your own boss, but you still have a job that is completely dependent on your ability to win proposals and deliver the work. When you stop working, the money stops coming in.

A true business can turn a profit without you. When the original McDonald's burger joint closed, did the company go out of business? No! When Jeff Bezos relinquished his responsibilities as Amazon's CEO, did packages stop arriving at your doorstep? Of course not! That is because these are real businesses with true entrepreneurs at the helm.

‖‖‖‖‖‖‖‖‖‖‖‖‖‖‖‖‖‖‖‖‖ **FINANCIAL FAST TRACK FACT** ‖‖‖‖‖‖‖‖‖‖‖‖‖‖‖‖‖‖‖‖‖

BILLIONAIRE BUSINESS OWNERS DOMINATE MONEY THROUGH THE POWER OF LEVERAGE.

Here's a secret: Entrepreneurs aren't doers. They are people who get things done in three fundamental ways:

1) **Empowering:** Entrepreneurs develop and train the right people to accomplish the mission.

2) **Automating:** Entrepreneurs create the right structure and systems to dominate in their respective fields.

3) **Leveraging:** Entrepreneurs connect via strategic relationships to get more done faster.

These primary means make you money whether you work, sleep, go fishing, or take your wife on vacation. Yes, even while you're in your underwear. This is the way you master your money and take dominion over your finances. If your business can't do that, it's not a business. It is a glorified job that you happen to own.

The first thing I coach my business owner clients to do is develop a "Stop Doing List." (To learn more about this get your free ticket to my Leaders of Destiny Virtual Experience at LeadersofDestinyExperience.com.) You need to establish a business that works regardless of your participation. Until you do, your prospects and impact will be tied to your availability which is limited.

If your business cannot produce unless you are present, why own a business? You don't start a company to become a glorified employee. You start or buy a business for four basic reasons:

1) To make a difference.

2) To create positive cash flow.

3) To sell it for a massive profit.

4) To leave it to your children.

A note about selling your business: you will never make as much money running a profitable business as you will selling it.

Steer Clear of Business Fear

In the Industrial Age, people were taught to avoid risk, the ultimate risk being business ownership. The business-fear crowd is quick to remind you that roughly 80 percent of startups fail. Of course, they never talk about the percentage of retired senior citizens who live on Social Security and pay for their medication by working as Walmart door greeters.

Many startups fail because many new owners lack the information and skills necessary to win. Even if they graduated from high school, trade school, or college, few of them learned successful entrepreneurship.

Imagine that you wanted to fly an airplane. Would you start out by jumping into a Boeing 777 cockpit and pushing buttons until you found one that worked? No! Would you invite your spouse and children along while you get the hang of flying? Of course not.

Yet, that is exactly what many people do when they start a business. They have no experience in the field, have not educated themselves or developed the necessary skills, and haven't hired a coach to get them there faster.

I have seen this pattern again and again. It's the reason I never push people to quit their jobs tomorrow and launch their businesses. What they need, and what you need, is preparation. Start by spending your evenings and weekends developing your confidence and competency. Read books by successful entrepreneurs. Learn about business, particularly *your* business. Then, when you are ready, pull the trigger with massive, intelligent action.

End the Journey of Broke and Dream Again

Remember: if you are struggling to make money, you are focused on doing it the hard way. You might even be oblivious to the possibility of making big money easily.

Is the voice in your head still saying, *Fast money sounds good, but I need a steady job with a paycheck I can count on*? You have already seen that your premise is false. This is the worst time for employees and the best time to be a business owner.

If the lie in your head hasn't scared you off, other people's voices might. Belittling remarks are some people's way of venting their secret fears and taking you down a peg.

- » "You're not thinking realistically."
- » "That is too much to expect."
- » "You need to calm down."
- » "You're working too hard."
- » "What gives you the right?"

» "Get off your high horse and fly under the radar."

» "Just get a regular job!"

If that is what you are hearing, it is coming from those who are uneasy with greatness and very comfortable with mediocrity. Average people feel exposed around massive action-takers. When they criticize you, you are probably on the right track. They want you to have a job for the same reason that you wanted one: it is what we were taught.

What you need is not a job but a dream. Remember that a salary is the drug they give you to forget your dream. The J-O-B you are so afraid to lose is your Journey of Broke. There is no job security. *Period.*

If you work for someone else, that person or entity sets your hours, controls your raises, decides when you have earned a promotion, determines how much time off you can take, and is free to fire you at will. If your idea of safety is being at the mercy of a person or corporation, you have been misled. The moment the business folds, starts layoffs, or fires you, you can kiss your "secure" paycheck goodbye. It might have been regular while it lasted, but it never was reliable.

It's time to dream again. It is time to build your business.

Not sure where to start? Take a good look at your current industry or the industry into which you want to transition. Gain knowledge and experience. Be intentional about growing your confidence and competence. Don't jump in the cockpit without preparing yourself to fly.

Next, look for big problems to solve. What problems have you faced? What problems are people around you discussing? Ask to meet with key decision makers. Ask about the three problems that keep them up at night. These clues can take you from the Journey of Broke to your Financial Fast Track.

Are you ready to mind your own business? Good! In the next chapter I will share the #1 strategy I share with my private clients, so they can accelerate their business success. So, strap in. You are going somewhere!

· · · · · · · · · ·

FINANCIAL FAST TRACK COACHING

The following are the three biggest questions you can ask about your financial future. Consider your answers carefully.

1) Am I looking for the opportunity that will provide abundance for me and my family for the rest of our lives? What are my requirements for that opportunity?

2) Have I found the right opportunity yet? What is my next step?

3) Am I investing time each week to seek that opportunity?

If your answers are "No" or "I don't know," you have work to do. It's possible that you have been waiting for a miracle. But miracles often appear as mentors. Ask, seek, and knock (Matthew 7:7). Ask people in the know for the help you need. Intentionally seek the right vehicle for your financial future. And knock on the door of opportunity.

4) When developing your business, ask yourself the following four questions. Take as much time as you need to answer them fully.

1. How can I do something *better*?

2. How can I do something *cheaper*?

3. How can I do something *faster*?

4. How can I do something *new*?

13

THE SOLOMON STRATEGY

Soon after I muted my critics' voices, dropped the financial mythology, and committed to the Financial Fast Track, I discovered something astounding: the abundance of scriptures about creating wealth.

We've all seen "refrigerator verses" pertaining to money. What we need, however, is to study the Scriptures in depth and find the truth about generational wealth. When my financial crisis came, I was desperate for guidance. Ethereal language was not going to cut it. My credit cards were maxed out, and I was dead broke.

My only question was, "What can I do?"

I remember attending a three-day conference with a popular Christian personality you have probably seen on television. He pitched the conference as an "intensive" for gaining influence and favor. After three days of eight-hour meetings, I was more than disappointed. The topic of money never came up.

If you want to have influence and favor with others, money is an issue. If you aren't on the fast track to financial success, you are like the wise man in Ecclesiastes 9:15: although he had the wisdom to save his city, no one remembered him. Verse 16 says that "the poor man's wisdom is despised, and his words are not heard."

Let's be honest about how the world works. You might be the wisest and most spiritual Christian in your city, but without wealth, you will never make the impact you are called to make.

This truth became the clearest during my hardest times, and it compelled my quest for wealth. I found the answers I needed, not within the walls of the church but within the pages of Scripture. What surprised me most was finding that my dream from God was not only possible but was in the Book!

That's right. My dream of being a speaker, author, coach and thought leader was confirmed in 1 Kings 10. There, I saw something I had long overlooked about King Solomon.

> *Then she gave the king one hundred and twenty talents of gold, spices in great quantity, and precious stones. There never again came such abundance of spices as the queen of Sheba gave to King Solomon. . . . The weight of gold that came to Solomon yearly was six hundred and sixty-six talents of gold, besides that from the traveling merchants, from the income of traders, from all the kings of Arabia, and from the governors of the country. —1 Kings 10:10, 14–15*

Earlier, I mentioned Solomon's work as a consultant to international leaders. However, until I was buried in bad debt and living at my mother-in-law's, I missed that important detail. When desperation drove me to search the Scriptures, Solomon's strategy dawned on me. He built an expert empire. *I thought, Why didn't I see that before?*

Solomon was the first one in Scripture to model the pivot from being a generalist (someone who can talk about many topics but has mastered none) to starting his own expert industry with his wisdom message. What is the expert industry? It's an industry of caring people who share with the world their wisdom, advice, solutions, insights, systems, frameworks, and coaching skills—and get paid handsomely for it.

Yes! You can get paid for sharing the insider knowledge and how-to information that helps other people succeed. In fact, my mission is to inspire and instruct others on how to fulfill their God-given assignments, improve their lives, and achieve their goals.

Do the Queen of Sheba's gifts still seem extravagant, at least in terms of numbers? She was no fool. The extremity of her giving indicates the value she saw in what Solomon offered, which was his wisdom and expertise. That was of incalculable worth to her. Therefore, her expenditure was not exorbitant at all. It was good business.

Keep in mind that his expert empire was only one of Solomon's income streams, and the Queen of Sheba wasn't his only client.

Solomon's Timeless Strategy

The kings of Tyre and Arabia, and the Queen of Sheba sought Solomon's wisdom. There were no Zoom calls or texts. They had to travel to Jerusalem to meet him. No doubt, they arrived with hard questions. The answers that seemed so simple to him came to their ears as revelation.

People in every millennium need wisdom. Therefore, Solomon's ancient strategy still works. So, while people around me chirped about getting "a real job," God's Word spelled out a better way—and today's technology makes it even more viable than it was in Solomon's day.

Once I saw the light, I committed to becoming what I call an *info-preneur*. You already know that entrepreneurism is the vehicle most suited for the Financial Fast Track. However, info-preneurism is the route I recommend above all others.

Info-preneurs are business owners who present, market, and/or sell original information or the information of other experts. They package, promote, and provide instruction, inspiration, or special-interest content. There is no better way to reach millionaire status today.

Savvy info-preneurs focus on five products or services that are inexpensive to create and deliver. Therefore, they have higher profit margins than almost any product or service. Here are the top five that I recommend:

1) Books
2) Speeches (speaking engagements)
3) Coaching
4) Consulting
5) Courses

Consider the cost of writing and selling a booklet. At most, each unit runs a few dollars. What you can charge depends on the value of the content. I have paid $10 for books that present a general overview of a particular topic. But I paid thousands of dollars for a manual that lays out step-by-step instructions on growing and scaling my business. As valuable as the content is, the three-ring binder and pages cost about three dollars. With that kind of profit margin, there is no better opportunity on the planet.

When you become an info-preneur, you position yourself to impact your immediate area and potentially the globe. In return, the world pays you handsomely for providing the wisdom it needs. That is exactly what King Solomon did: he shared from his base of knowledge and experience, and he made a fortune.

‖‖‖‖‖‖‖‖‖‖‖‖‖‖‖‖‖ **FINANCIAL FAST TRACK FACT** ‖‖‖‖‖‖‖‖‖‖‖‖‖‖‖‖‖

INFORMATION OFFERS THE HIGHEST PROFIT MARGINS ON THE PLANET.

The info-preneur opportunity is the easiest and most cost-effective in history. Instead of building widgets, you use your mind to manufacture intellectual product. Or you share what you have learned from others. I'm not talking about stealing people's intellectual property. That is neither scriptural nor ethical. I'm talking about acknowledging and sharing your work and the work of others through licensing agreements.

The outstanding advantage of info-preneurism is that harvesting information does not require astronomical tooling, production, or labor costs. Instead, you deliver paper or pixels and are paid for the informational and educational value they contain.

Today, you can create a book that requires nothing but your time. You can write it in an app like Google Docs, save it as a PDF, and sell it as an e-book. There are no printing costs or shipping fees, and when the product is sold, the funds drop directly into your bank account.

The twenty-first century ease of delivery and speed of money have made it possible for countless authors to self-publish and reap the rewards of info-preneurism. In my 83K Academy, I teach a framework for writing a great book in only seven full days. Yes—*seven days*.

You could go a step further than e-books by using a print-on-demand option. In that case, you would write the book in your app, lay it out, so it looks like a book, and email the file to the printer. In a couple of weeks, your book can be delivered to your clients' doorsteps. If you meet a minimum order quantity (as low as twenty-five books), you can have them shipped for a few bucks apiece.

You can use those books as business cards that help you line up speaking dates. Then, you can sell more books as product at those events. That's a lot of bang for your buck!

I often mail books to potential clients. I add a sticky note that says, "You haven't heard of me, but I've heard of you, and I believe I can help." I sign the note and add my phone number. For a few dollars to print and ship, I can land a $10,000 speaking opportunity or start a conversation for private coaching that garners $120,000.

What if you aren't a writer? No problem! You don't have to be Charles Dickens or Tony Robbins. All you need is information that other people will pay to have. And if you don't want to write a book, just speak one.

That's right! Use the voice memo app on your phone and use a voice transcription service to turn the recording into a book. You're not looking to become a literary figure. You are positioning yourself as an expert. Having a real book creates a public profile that says you "wrote the book" on your subject.

I often ask conference attendees to raise their hands if they have a book inside them. About 90 percent of adults say that they do. I guarantee you that the information and experience in each of their heads is enough to generate a lifetime stream of income.

The same is true of what you know. With the right positioning, your new book can be the launchpad of your information empire!

If you have one idea, concept, or skill that other people want to understand, you are by definition an expert. If you doubt what I'm saying, check the beginning of most success books. They almost always describe an author who was once poor, overweight, ugly, depressed, alone, or addicted. Then the book explains how some miracle (usually the miracle of information) turned disaster into a success story.

Your fortune is buried within your story! Through books, newsletters, courses, coaching, or consulting you can share that story with people who desperately need what you have learned. God wastes nothing. Every loss and every win can become a stream of income for your good and His glory.

You have heard the phrase: "What doesn't kill you makes you stronger." Well, I have a better one: What doesn't kill you can make you richer.

FINANCIAL FAST TRACK FACT

WHAT DOESN'T KILL YOU CAN MAKE YOU RICHER.

Fishing for a Fortune

When I was a kid, I loved fishing trips with my grandpa. His approach was simple. He always stopped at the bait shop, jumped into our rented boat, and got us off to where we would find some fish.

We had a blast every time. Of course, the first day always seemed like a failure. The lake was big. It took time to scope out which fish were biting, where they were, and which bait they liked.

After that long first day, Grandpa would settle into the cabin for a game of poker. That's when I would take the boat and fish for information from the lake itself and from other people.

It paid off! By the end of the second day, we would fill large trash cans with crappie, bluegill, bass, and northern pike. We had the best time and enjoyed eating fresh Indiana fish together. But I learned something from our trips that serves me to this day.

The essential skills of the info-preneur are a lot like the ones Grandpa and I needed on those fishing trips. Let's look at the top three.

Skill #1: Targeting Schools of Hungry Fish

To sell your information, you must identify a market and its viability. In fishing terms, your market is a school of fish. Are there lots of fish in the school? Are its numbers growing or declining? Are the fish easy to find and identify? Are they hungry or just snacking? Which bait starts a feeding frenzy? And are you prepared to catch those fish?

Skill #2: Creating Irresistible Bait

The feeding frenzy you need to succeed is largely about presentation. Offer your expertise in a way that is irresistible to the fish. Human needs and desires don't change. People have always needed God, power, money, health, relationships, and self-esteem. Your job is to meet those needs and desires by offering information in ways that tap into universal truths. In fishing terms, make sure you use the right bait at the right time.

Skill #3: Catching Lifetime Clients

Once you land a client, retaining the client becomes your goal. If you continue to add value, your clients will be loyal. With a thousand loyal clients, you have an information empire. If each spends $100 a year for your information, you have made $100,000. If they spend $1,000 a year, you have a million-dollar information empire. The secret is to keep feeding the "fish." Do that, and they will swim in your lake, potentially for a lifetime.

Now let's add some tips to your three essential skills. Remember that you are building something of value, an empire that is not only sustainable but expanding. Fine-tune your process, take meaningful action, and your results will be significant.

1) Choose a subject that matches your gifting, passion, experience, or expertise. This could be a career field in which you have worked, a cause you want to promote, a challenge you have overcome, a skill you have developed, or a hobby that you share with others. The more you know, the more you have to offer from Day 1.

2) Locate the hungriest fish in the lake. Do your due diligence. Use Google, mailing-list brokers, and resources such as Who's Mailing What! to find the schools of fish that are hungriest for what you know.

3) Discover the best bait. This is your market research. Study what successful fishermen have been doing in your waters. Talk to prospective clients. Find out what ideal clients are hungry to learn. Learn how they want your content packaged. Ask questions.

4) Create your unique bait. Finding the right bait is important, but we often forget to make it unique. Ask your target fish what they don't like about your competitors. What would they add to your competitor's product? What would they leave out? Ask them to describe their perfect product. Then assemble it for them.

5) Test the bait. In marketing, everything begins as a test. Without it, you lack feedback as to whether the marketplace is hungry for your bait. Once you design the bait that has proven results, it's time to create consistent advertising that makes your fish want to feed!

6) Roll out the campaign. You can launch a successful product that leads to multiple products with the same information. That means books, audiobooks, newsletters, courses, group coaching, private coaching, and consulting. Hungry fish want to eat more than once, and they want a menu of presentations.

7) Enjoy the info-preneurial life. Work from home or from your favorite coffee shop. Share your experiences and expertise as only you can. Carve out a better life.

Solomon's strategy is truly timeless, and the way forward is easy to grasp. You already have something to offer, and it's probably staring you in the face. So go fishing! Everything we covered in this chapter and the previous chapters will point you in the right direction.

Yet there is more—much more!

· · · · · · · · · ·

FINANCIAL FAST TRACK COACHING

Like a fish that's been swimming in its lake a long time, you might not realize that you are "wet." What I mean is, your knowledge and experience are so familiar to you that you can overlook their value. Seeing your expertise with fresh eyes means seeing it through the needs of others. Then you will recognize what you have to offer.

1) If you have never hammered a nail, someone who has done it once is an expert in your mind. What have you learned that seems like common knowledge to you but might be "news" to someone without your experience?

2) What is the heart of your expertise? Consider it a kind of river; then, look for the tributaries that flow from it. How can they add to your information empire?

3) After reading this chapter, can you see yourself writing a book? Why or why not? Examine your "nots" and decide whether you will sacrifice your dream for them.

14

MY $83,000-A-MONTH SECRET: WHAT'S NEXT FOR YOU?

The poor and middle classes are being squeezed. Those in poverty have always suffered, but now the middle class is disappearing. Some members have migrated to higher income brackets. But stagnant wages, market uncertainties, and other factors are forcing other middle-income earners into the low-income pool.

For everyone still in the middle, only one question remains: *On which end of the disappearing act will I land?*

This issue motivates me to do what I do, teach what I teach, and write the books I write. It compels me to help others imagine and accomplish the $83,000-a-month secret that has changed my life. As the founder of the America's #1 Confidence Coach brand, an Amazon best-selling author, and a television personality, I've spoken before millions of people on the largest stages in the world. I've shared my story because I know what it's like to be squeezed—and I know how amazing it is to live your dream.

You know my story. You can probably relate to it in some way. Things started out great for me. My dream of becoming a professional speaker was finally happening. Then in 2001, the Twin Towers were toppled, and so was my business. With my events cancelled and all income lost, my wife and I got buried in credit card debt. We did what you should never have to do: we used one card to pay the next until we maxed out thirty-nine cards. That's how we survived . . . until our house of cards came crashing down.

We were forced to sell our stuff and move into my mother-in-law's tiny spare bedroom with a bed, a card table, and a suitcase of clothes stashed in the only available corner of the room. It was our rock bottom.

I confess that it was my mother-in-law who told me to "get off my butt and get a *real* job!" She always had a way with words. But, if you had met me in 2002, you would have agreed that I was the world's biggest failure. And I wouldn't have argued with you.

One afternoon, I managed to scrape together enough change from the couch cushions to get two McDonald's hamburgers—singles, not doubles. It was our first time eating out since I lost my business—a real treat.

On the way to the golden arches, I saw a man on the corner with a cardboard sign that said, "Homeless. Hungry. Any little bit helps. God bless."

I thought, "Wow. The only difference between that man and me is a piece of cardboard. I could be on the corner next to him tomorrow."

Only the lump in my throat kept me from crying.

The next day my mother-in-law took my wife shopping to get her out of the house for a bit. I was left alone with my thoughts and God.

It was my breaking point.

Sitting at the breakfast nook, I cried out to God in the ugliest, sloppiest way you can imagine. "What is wrong with me?" I shouted. "Why am I stuck here?"

I sensed God speaking into my spirit, as clear as day. *Keith, do you really want to know?* Whatever God was about to say would probably be hard to swallow. I knew it was a significant moment . . . my moment of truth.

Keith, you lack confidence. I wasn't even sure that was biblical, but Hebrews 10:35 showed me that it was. It says, "Therefore, do not cast away your confidence, which has great reward."

Reinvigorated by this revelation, I invited my coach to meet with my wife and me.

We were dreaming about the future, strategizing about what I was going to do next with my business. Then I asked this simple question: "What is my greatest strength?"

Instantly, my coach replied. "Whenever I'm around you, Keith, I feel more confident. I can't explain it. I just feel it."

You know the rest. My goal was to fix my own confidence, then champion the message of confidence for others. Through that journey, I became a world-class expert, an info-preneur in the making—someone who gets paid to help other people succeed.

Today, if you search the term *confidence coach* online, you will find hundreds of people who took my advice and entered the expert industry. My message, and now their messages, continue spreading to the masses.

Do the Millionaire Math

No other business can get you to the million-dollar mark faster and for such a small investment as the info-preneur business. You read in previous chapters about the nine-to-five trap, the slow, sinking boat to China.

It doesn't work. It's too slow and out of your control.

There's another problem. Most people say they want to be millionaires, but they never do the math. To earn a million dollars a year (or $83,333 a month) you need to make $19,000 a week, or $2,700 a day.

Warren Buffett did the math and said, "If you don't find a way to make money while you sleep, you will work until you die."[87]

He's right. You need passive income that flows at all hours, no matter where you are or what you are doing. Your job can't do that.

Have you been climbing the corporate ladder only to discover that you are stuck on a forty-year treadmill? You need to get on the Financial Fast Track, and you need the right vehicle: the information industry.

Are you wondering how to break into that space? Are you thinking, *I don't have anything to say*?

Let me jog your memory.

At some point in your life, you have faced adversity. Odds are, you have overcome some type of challenge. Have you seen someone struggling and thought, *If they only knew what I know*? That's it—the beginning of your million-dollar expert empire.

By now you know that I'm not trafficking in theory. What I am sharing is what I have lived. More importantly, I know that you can live it too. Start where you are, with what I call your Global Success Story. Notice that it has three "legs."

87 Warren Buffet > Quotes > Quotable Quote, *Goodreads*, accessed October 18, 2021, https://www.goodreads.com/quotes/8760232-if-you-don-t-find-a-way-to-make-money-while.

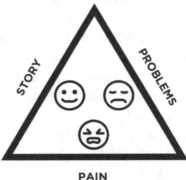

Leg #1: Your Story

People don't connect with you at the place of your successes. They connect with your failures and struggles. So, what was the greatest struggle you ever faced? Mine was losing my confidence at my life's lowest point.

When you survive your struggle, someone else needs to hear your story. In fact, many people will gladly pay to learn how you got through it. Sharing your story can radically impact their lives.

You share the value of your journey in three ways:

1) Story—what you have lived in the past that has made you the person you are today

2) Knowledge—the things you have learned from studying a particular subject

3) Experience—what you have earned by paying the price of time, successes, and mistakes

Leg #2: Your Problem

Another type of opportunity comes from solving a problem that you have faced. Instead of your greatest struggle, think this time about a one-time, isolated situation that you overcame. Can you identify the problem and explain how you solved it? It might involve a family issue or a career challenge. It might even be related to a hobby. The "problem" path is a lucrative one for the info-preneur.

Let #3: Your Pain

The third area to consider is your pain. What was the greatest pain you ever suffered? It's easy to get stuck in pain because longstanding issues can be hard to shake. Think about a disappointment you experienced. Maybe it was a divorce. Or maybe you suffered an injury. People around the world are experiencing similar challenges, and they need your help!

The Global Story Triangle is about the things every human being experiences. Your greatest opportunity lies within the struggle, problem, and pain you endure. As your coach, I want to help you maximize that opportunity and create a solution that you can package, promote, and sell—not only to make a fortune, but to make a difference.

Remember: Debt is not your problem; income is. And an information business is the answer. This is not only the solution I offer my Financial Fast Track clients; it is the path that changed my life.

Through my 83K Academy, I have helped many students get fast results in their speaking, coaching, and consulting businesses. I have helped stay-at-home moms retire their husbands. I have seen pastors replace their church salaries and scale beyond the best money they ever made. I have also seen retirees launch consulting practices that earn more than their forty-year careers ever did.

I admit, it's a little strange to stand on this side of success, as I do today. From the outside, I didn't look like someone you would pick to succeed, much less be a best-selling author, speaker, and coach.

*I was the **author** who couldn't read or write after failing kindergarten.*
*I was the **speaker** who overcame crippling stage fright.*
*I was the **coach** who had a mountain of debt and no money.*
*I was the **consultant** who had no clients of my own.*
*I was the **course creator** who couldn't finish college.*

So, how was my turnaround possible? It came down to a divine moment—a moment of realization and decision.

This is your moment. You've always dreamed of helping others and making a million dollars. For years, you've played the *what if* game in your mind. You've envisioned speaking on stages all over the world, publishing that best seller and working with impressive clients to coach them to greater success.

But have you done the math? Do you know what's next? Are you interested in an intensive, ninety-day coaching experience? Would some powerful trade secrets help? How about practical new courses, brand coaching, and more?

============== **FINANCIAL FAST TRACK FACT** ==============

DESIRE REVEALS DESIGN. A FISH DESIRES TO SWIM BECAUSE GOD DESIGNED IT TO SWIM.

Today's Decision Is Tomorrow's Reality

It is time to stop talking about success and start creating it. Your life moves at the speed of your decisions. On the other side of obedience are the millions of lives that will be transformed by your message. The wealth that follows is simply God's reward for serving His people. Commit to a life of service to others, and you will not only make a difference—you will make a fortune.

If you apply for acceptance into the 83K Academy, either I or a member of my team will review your application. Due to the one-on-one nature of the program, only twelve students will be selected per quarter.

I am so thankful that I could put this book into your hands. It has been a labor of love to provide you with actionable insights and the confidence to take quantum leaps like the ones that transformed and continue to transform my life.

Now, I would be off-the-charts honored to serve you through our 83K Academy and its intensive, interactive, and hands-on approach. If you're ready to enter the Financial Fast Track and build your expert empire, visit 83KAcademy.com and apply now!

But whatever your next step is, go ahead and take it on the fast track.

CPSIA information can be obtained
at www.ICGtesting.com
Printed in the USA
LVHW051629030222
709905LV00006B/26